Large as Life

A musical

Book by Richard Harris

Music by Keith Strachan

Lyrics by Richard Harris and Keith Strachan

Samuel French — London
New York - Toronto - Hollywood

© 2001 by Wishbone Limited and Keith Strachan

This play is fully protected under the Copyright Laws of the British Commonwealth of Nations, the United States of America and all countries of the Berne and Universal Copyright Conventions.

All rights including Stage, Motion Picture, Radio, Television, Public Reading, and Translation into Foreign Languages, are strictly reserved.

> **No part of this publication may lawfully be reproduced in ANY form or by any means — photocopying, typescript, recording (including video-recording), manuscript, electronic, mechanical, or otherwise—or be transmitted or stored in a retrieval system, without prior permission.**

SAMUEL FRENCH LTD, 52 FITZROY STREET, LONDON W1T 5JR, or their authorized agents, issue licences to amateurs to give performances of this play on payment of a fee. **This fee is subject to contract and subject to variation at the sole discretion of Samuel French Ltd.**

Licences for amateur performances are issued subject to the understanding that it shall be made clear in all advertising matter that the audience will witness an amateur performance; that the names of the authors of the plays shall be included on all programmes; and that the integrity of the authors' work will be preserved.

> **The publication of this play does not imply that it is necessarily available for performance by amateurs or professionals, either in the British Isles or Overseas. Amateurs and professionals considering a production are strongly advised in their own interests to apply to the appropriate agents for consent before starting rehearsals or booking a theatre or hall.**

ISBN 0 573 08114 X

The Professional Rights in this musical are controlled by The Agency (London) Ltd, 24 Pottery Lane, Holland Park, London, W11 4LZ

Large As Life

First produced, under the title *Baby Love*, at the Thorndike Theatre, Leatherhead, in association with the Nuffield Theatre, Southampton and Bill Kenwright Ltd, on 23rd February 1993. The cast was as follows:

Chris	Jason Hetherington
Caro	Amanda Garwood
Don	David McAllister
Helen	Belinda Sinclair
Patrick	Simon Slater
Jan	Tessa Burbridge
Liz	Joanna Munro
Stuart	David Cardy
Vicki	Susie McKenna
Paul	Benjamin Fellows
Lorraine	Clare Woodgate

Directed by **Patrick Sandford**
Designed by **Robin Don**
Musical Direction by **Caroline Humphris**
Lighting design by **Jason Taylor**

CHARACTERS

Caro, the classic blonde English rose, mezzo-soprano, mid 20s
Chris, an Anglo-Irish charmer, light tenor, mid 20s

Lorraine, looks little more than a child, soprano, 18
Paul, of a white mother and black father—like his wife, looks little more than a child, tenor, 19

Helen, attractive, alto, 40
Don, baritone, late 40s

Vicki, voluptuous, untidy, mezzo-soprano, late 20s
Stuart, bass-baritone, late 20s

Jan, pre-Raphaelite, mezzo-soprano, mid 20s
Patrick, earnest, tenor, early 30s

Liz, angry with the world, mezzo-soprano, late 20s

MUSICAL NUMBERS

ACT I

1	**All On Our Way**	The Company
2	**Mood Swing Waltz**	Jan & Patrick
3	**In the Club**	The Women
4	**Would You Miss Me?**	Vicki & Stuart
5	**I Don't Need It**	Liz
6	**Oh The Pain**	The Women
7	**If Only**	Don
8	**Look at Me**	Caro & Chris
9	**I Can Feel It**	The Company

ACT II

10	**Ladies in Waiting**	The Women & Patrick
11	**Live Your Own Life**	Liz & Lorraine
12	**My Dad**	Paul
13	**Look at Me**	Don, Helen, Lorraine, Paul, Caro, Chris
14	**Ask Me**	Caro & Chris
15	**Nothing to Do with Wendy**	Helen
16	**It's Starting**	The Company
17	**The Birth**	The Company
	All On Our Way (curtain call)	

Music

Because of the economic restraints of commercial theatre this musical is scored for only four players - Piano/MD, Keyboard 2, Keyboard 3 and bass guitar. There is also a Vocal book available. Keyboards 2 and 3 play a variety of sounds, including drums and percussion on keyboard. In amateur circles it is conceivable that this may present problems as the sounds and instruments I've scored are quite specific. However, I've tried to organise the score in such a way that there is a degree of flexibility in the choice of instruments. I've indicated in each band part the basic requirements and trust this will not cause any problems.

Of course, it shouldn't be overlooked that the musical will work perfectly well with piano only.

Keith Strachan

The Piano/MD part, orchestral parts and Vocal books are available on hire from the Music Department of Samuel French Ltd.

ACT I

As the CURTAIN *rises all the company is on stage. Frozen in the moment where each of the women has told her partner the news*

At the same time the sound of a heartbeat plus music ... and then a female voice announces

Female Voice "First of all let us examine exactly what you're getting into..."

All On Our Way

Caro	I heard today
Vicki	On its way
Patrick	A baby
Paul	Baby
Lorraine	Baby
Don	Are you sure?
Helen	Yes, I'm sure
Jan	Very sure
Women & Patrick	It's on its way

Paul	What did he say?
Stuart	You OK?
Helen	A baby
Paul	Baby
Liz	Baby?
Don	Say again
Chris	Tell me when
Liz	Count to ten
	And try to smile
Jan	In a while I'll be...
Chris	Soon be three
	You and me
Chris & Caro	And baby
Patrick	Baby
Helen	Baby
Don	When's it due?
Stuart	I love you
Paul	Say it's true

Women   We're on our way
All   Happy day
Men   A baby

The following sections of dialogue are underscored by a chorus of "Baby, Baby"... All freeze except Chris and Caro. Chris gives Caro a small bunch of freesias

Chris (*kissing Caro*) You're a very clever girl.
Caro (*so happy*) Do you know what day it is?
Chris Err ... the anniversary of the Battle of the Bulge.
Caro It's exactly a year to the day since we first met.
Chris How the hell do you remember these things?
Caro Because they're important to me... Chris ... we're having a baby... (*she embraces him*) isn't it wonderful?
Chris It's terrific.

They hold the embrace

(*Breaking the embrace*) Hey... I'd better phone my mother...
Caro Tell her ... tell her properly, Chris...
Chris Course I will. (*He embraces her again*) She'll be thrilled to bits.

They hold the embrace

Chris & Caro Didn't we
Both agree
A baby?

	Liz	Baby
Did the deed	**Lorraine**	Baby
And indeed		
We succeeded		
Always do		
Nothing new	**All**	A baby

All freeze except Don and Helen

Don A baby? (*He sits on their bed*) Are you sure?
Helen Don... I don't have to go through with it—I mean if you're really unhappy...

He stands and embraces her

Act I

Don (*trying to sound enthusiastic*) It's the best news I've had in years and I'm thrilled to bits. (*But he can't resist*) It's just a hell of a surprise, that's all. (*He smiles at the sudden thought*) Wait until Wendy finds out … the thought of *me* changing nappies again.

Helen …You won't tell her, will you, Don? I mean not yet. Not until we're sure.

Don Of course I won't tell her. (*He continues to embrace her, smiling … and we see concern in his face*)

	Tell me how
	Did we start
	This baby?
Patrick	Baby
Caro	Baby
Helen	Look at me
Helen & Don	You and me
Helen	Could it be that…?
Don	I mean how?
Helen & Don	I mean wow!

All freeze except Jan and Patrick who are looking intently at a pregnancy test tube

Patrick	OK, so now we can plan…
Jan	Plan ahead
Patrick	I intend to participate
	As much as possible

Jan (*holding up a book*) *The Participating Father.*
Jan & Patrick (*toasting Jan with the tube*) Congratulations.

Jan & Patrick	And of course
	The baby
Patrick	Did the test
Jan	It turned pink
Patrick	So I think…
Jan	It's a baby
Patrick	Baby
Lorraine	Baby

Liz (*speaking*) Maybe!
Jan & Patrick Now there's no doubt
 That our baby is on its way

All freeze except Liz who speaks into a phone

Liz Cystitis. I went to the doctor with cystitis and she came back with a white face and said.

Other Women (*singing*) You're pregnant
Liz I had no idea, I just thought I was a bit—late.

All freeze except Stuart and Vicki

Stuart Hallo doll, you look beautiful, where are the kids?
Vicki Fast asleep, thank God.

Stuart sits

Stuart (*taking out a copy of an evening paper*) Anything happened?
Vicki The fence fell down.
Stuart Oh yeah? Anything else?
Vicki Yes, there is as it happens: I'm pregnant.
Stuart (*discarding the newspaper*) When?
Vicki Musta been the night of your brother's birthday party.
Stuart You are, you're beautiful, beautiful. (*He pulls her on to his lap and embraces her*)
Vicki (*looking over his shoulder*) What can I do with the man?
Men A baby

All freeze except Liz

Liz I didn't tell my fella until the next day. I must admit he was incredibly supportive. Get rid of it, he said. (*She gives a sardonic little jerk of the head*) I got rid of him instead.
Some Are you sure?
Liz Sure of what?
Who the hell
Wants a baby?

Look at me
What of me?
What to do?
What of my career?

All freeze except Paul and Lorraine

Paul Well?
Lorraine Yes.

He whoops and they embrace excitedly

Lorraine Oh, he'll be so loved.

Act I

Paul Oh, he's a boy, is he?
Lorraine I don't care what he is as long as he's all right and he's like you.
Paul (*hugging her tighter*) I love you, Lorraine.
Lorraine I love you, Paul.
Paul I'll make a terrific dad, you'll see… (*but suddenly concerned*) here … sit down.
Lorraine (*smiling happily*) Not yet, silly.
Paul A baby… I can't wait! I want to tell the whole world. Do you know that?

She reaches up to take his hand

     I'm so proud
Paul & Lorraine Shout it loud
     Can't believe
     Just how I feel

All   We're on our way
     Ever near to the day
     When we'll understand
     The joys of parenthood
     We'll look and compare
     Be aware that everywhere
     Children are children
     Who would believe
     To conceive is a miracle
     I believe it
     We've achieved it
     Now there's no doubt
     No conceivable doubt
     We're on our way

All Except Liz & Don	And soon we'll find That nothing will be the same With yesterday left behind Tomorrow is on our mind	**Liz & Don**	Somehow things have got to change Nothing ventured nothing gained
Men	A journey begun So much to be done Together as one Regrets we have none We'll tell everyone	**Women**	Making all our plans Trying to see our way Doing all we can Each and every day Seeing what we see

> In another way
> Hearing what is said,
> go ahead
> Planning everything
> Nothing can be the same

All   We're all on our way
Jan Oh my God!

Patrick, Don and Paul look with concern at Jan, Helen and Lorraine. They, like Liz, are exhibiting various symptoms of early pregnancy. Helen has the flushes and will fan herself. Chris and Caro remain immune

Don & Patrick & Paul *What?*
All Women I feel sick.
Patrick Actually… I feel a bit queasy myself. (*Generally, to the other men*) Sharing is caring!

Paul and Patrick exit

Helen (*fanning herself furiously*) And if I'm so tired all the time, surely it means there must be something wrong with me.
Don (*brightly*) Tell you what Wendy used to do…
Helen Please … *please…*

They get into bed. We see Vicki and Stuart. Vicki is studying her wedding ring which is suspended on a length of cotton, Stuart is reading a specialist car magazine

Vicki I shall have to stop biting my nails.
Stuart You say that every time. Natasha.
Vicki Natasha?
Stuart What d'you think?

Vicki considers

Vicki No.
Stuart Well, if it's a boy, it's definitely Vincent.
Vicki How many more times, it's not gonna be a boy.
Stuart How can you be so sure?
Vicki Because I've not been so nauseous, have I? That is a well-known biological fact.

Act I

Stuart (*of the wedding ring*) I suppose that is, an'all.
Vicki (*moving across*) You think back to what I was like with Jeremy and then what I was like with Samantha. (*She calls*) Go to sleep!

A call of "Mum!" from offstage

What? Yeah, all right, in a minute.
Stuart What's she want?
Vicki A story.
Stuart I'll go. (*He makes to exit*)
Vicki Not that one about the wicked bookmaker, right?

He puts his arms around her from behind

Stuart I tell you this: you look really tasty when you're pregnant.
Vicki You mean I don't when I'm not.
Stuart You do—really tasty. I don't half love you, Victoria.
Vicki Yeah yeah yeah.
Stuart Say you love me.
Vicki Love you—OK?
Stuart Say it properly.
Vicki Go away, I'm busy.

But she makes no effort to move away as he keeps his arms around her

Stuart Get your mother round and we'll go out for a ride, waddaya think?
Vicki I think you've done enough damage for one season, don't you?
Stuart Waddaya think?
Vicki Tomorrow maybe.
Stuart I'm working late tomorrow… (*He kisses her neck*) Go on, go and get your mum. (*He makes for the exit*) I'm coming, I'm coming!

Stuart exits

Vicki stands for a moment, putting the ring back on her finger. She touches the ring, smiling fondly

Vicki (*to herself*) Silly sod, he is.

Pause. Then there is a sudden loud yell of fear and Helen jerks upright in the bed, having a nightmare. Don leaps out of bed, grabbing up a golf iron, thinking it's a burglar. But he realizes and will comfort Helen

Helen I'm sorry, I'm sorry…

Vicki exits

Don ...it's all right, it's all right... (*He continues to gently soothe away her fears*)
Helen I had the most horrible dream...
Don ...there, there...
Helen ...God, it was horrible... I should have thought about what having a baby at my age meant... I don't know how I'll cope if anything goes wrong...
Don ...hey hey hey hey... (*He gently turns her face towards him*) I love you.
Helen (*clinging to him like a child*) Oh, and I love you...

Pause. Through the following, Don is gently shushing her

Don You're bound to be all over the place until you've had the results of the test...
Helen ...Don, what if there *is* something wrong...?
Don ...There won't be anything wrong...
Helen ...then there are your children—I mean...
Don (*gently*) ...what about my children?
Helen I worry about them seeing a new baby as a, I don't know, a loss of love... I know how much they mean to you, I couldn't bear it if...
Don ...it'll be all right, I promise you.
Helen And Don... you haven't told their mother, have you, you haven't told Wendy, I mean I don't think we should tell anyone, not until we know for certain that everything's...

He puts a finger gently to her lips and then kisses her. This moment, and she holds him tight

Helen What's it like sleeping with an elderly primigravida?
Don Well, I'll tell you: it's not half bad.

A moment, he is embracing her playfully and turning off the light and they snuggle down into the bed

Helen I love you so much, I really do.

They remain in each other's arms for a moment and then Helen extricates herself and sits upright. During the following, Don sits upright, turns on the light, bewildered

(*With a complete change of tone*) There is one thing though, Don... I wish

you'd stop phoning me at the office, I have work to do, it really is very embarrassing having you phoning up every five minutes for a health report—I'm pregnant, I am not ill. And don't tell me how Wendy The Wonder Woman would have coped because I'm not interested.
Don I never said a word about...
Helen ...no, but you were going to. (*She gets out of bed*)
Don Helen, that is not true.
Helen Oh, yes, it is!
Don (*with his hands to his head*) Jesus!

She starts to wail. He moves to her

Don Why are you crying?
Helen I don't know why I'm crying... I'm just so ... emotional! (*She wails louder*)

Patrick and Jan enter. He reads from one of his many "Baby" books as he uses a spoon to eat from a bowl

Patrick "The first two months of pregnancy will often be characterised by violent swings in emotion caused by extreme hormonal activity..."

Helen wails louder. Don embraces her for comfort

Don I tell you what—why don't we...
Helen Oh, shut up! I'm sorry—I didn't mean that... (*She smothers him with kisses*) I don't know why I said it... (*A general plea*) What's happening to me?

Helen wails and exits and Don sighs and exits after her

Jan Oh, I don't think that applies to us, Patrick.
Patrick Not if we're careful to nurture a lifestyle that will give you peace of mind.
Jan We certainly don't want any worries projected on to the child.
Patrick Absolutely not. What's that you're eating?
Jan Carrot and chick-pea surprise.
Patrick Mmm, yummy.
Jan Because the thing is you see, Patrick ... if I can't cope, our child will resent me and become insecure and grow up into an anti-social monster—where are you going?
Patrick (*holding his handkerchief and speaking heavily through his nose*) I've got a cold coming—I think I'd better sleep in the other room.

Jan Why?
Patrick Because I don't want to risk infecting the baby.
Jan Sod the baby, I need a cuddle! (*She wails*)
Patrick Why are you crying?
Jan Because I will never again be alone with my husband!
Patrick Jan…
Jan …and why are you forcing me to eat this stuff? I hate it!
Patrick Jan…

Music

Jan You see, you're not listening!
Patrick I am listening, I promise. (*He tries to embrace her*)
Jan No!
Patrick What?

Song 2: Mood Swing Waltz

Jan	You never listen
Patrick	What?
Jan	See, you never listen
Patrick	Oh, I thought you said…
Jan	I love you
Patrick	But that's what I'm trying to say. OK?
Jan	No you don't, you hate me
Patrick	No!
Jan	Yes, because I'm ugly
Patrick	No.
Jan	Yes I am, I'm ugly and fat in the family way
Patrick	Not so.
Jan	Do we want this baby?
Patrick	Yes!
Jan	Why do you say maybe?
Patrick	Eh?
Jan	Maybe have a baby?
Patrick	Not maybe
Jan & Patrick	When it's on its way?
Jan	OK, tell me that you love me
Patrick	Yes!
Jan	Don't care if you love me
Patrick	No!
Jan	Don't care if we…
Patrick	OK then
Jan	OK then

Act I

Patrick & Jan OK, OK!

The music continues under

Jan Ummm...
Patrick Yes?
Jan Nothing.
Patrick Oh.
Jan You never listen
Patrick What?
Jan See, you never listen
Patrick Eh? But you just said
Jan I love you
Patrick But that's what I'm saying
Patrick & Jan Of course
Jan OK, I tell you what I fancy
Patrick Oh?
Jan Fancy some spaghetti
Patrick Now?
Jan Freshly cooked
Patrick Spaghetti?
Jan (*in a cod Italian accent*) Don't forgetti the bolognaise sauce

Patrick OK
Jan I really want this baby
Patrick Yes?
Jan No, I want some ice cream
Patrick Right.
Jan Or there again
Patrick Surprise me
Jan Don't despise me, don't be angry with me
Patrick I'm not!!
Jan Yes you are, you're angry
Patrick No!
Jan Just because I'm hungry
Patrick No!!
Jan Yes you are, you're...
Patrick OK then!
Jan OK then.
Jan & Patrick OK, OK!

The music continues under

Patrick Did you say something?

Jan Sorry?
Patrick My mistake.
Jan Huh. Now you ignore me
Patrick Who?
Jan You! You make me sore
Patrick Me?
Jan Yes, cos you ignore me
Patrick OK if you really insist
Jan My God.
Patrick Now you've made me
Jan Angry
Patrick You? (*singing*) Every day you're
Jan Happy
Patrick Well, (*singing*) I'm so glad you're happy
Jan Well, I'm not I'm completely depressed

Patrick My God, (*singing*) now you're like your
Jan Mother, (*speaking*) say it.
Patrick So much like your
Jan & Patrick Mother
Jan Aahh!
Patrick I see why your father would rather
Jan Take care what you say
Patrick I'm sorry. (*Singing*) I didn't
Jan Mean that?
Patrick No, (*singing*) I didn't mean that
Jan Well, (*singing*) what's the point of…
Patrick OK then
Jan OK then
Patrick & Jan OK, OK!

> We are dancing the
> Mood swing waltz
> While our minds are making their
> Somersaults

Jan I'm not nice.
Patrick You have faults.
Jan Thanks! No!
Patrick What?
Jan Is it genetic?
Patrick What?
Jan Why I'm so frenetic?
Patrick No.

Act I

Jan	The baby will…
Patrick	…Forget it…
Jan	…It might be
Patrick	That's just not the way
Jan	I feel…
Patrick	Thing is not to panic
Jan	Feel absolutely manic!
Patrick	Look, try to be specific
Jan	Terrific!
Patrick	What else can I say?

Jan I see. (*Singing*) Now you want to hurt me
Patrick No
Jan (*coyly*) Never want to love me
Patrick Oh, (*singing*) come and let me hold you
  I've told you
Patrick & Jan I love you
Jan This way
Patrick (*seductively*) That's nice.
Jan Have to use the toilet
Patrick Great! Always have to
Patrick & Jan Spoil it!
Patrick Me?
Jan You're the one that…
Patrick OK then
Jan OK then
Patrick & Jan OK, OK! OK!?

Don and Helen enter, each sipping from a breakfast cup. Helen is holding a letter

Helen I've had a letter from the hospital. I've got my first appointment. (*She reads*) "Be prepared to wait for at least three hours".
Don Don't forget to take a good book. (*He kisses her briefly and takes her cup*)

Don exits

And we are in the ante-natal clinic. There are various notices—including one which reads "Drink Plenty Of Water For The Scan"

All the women and Patrick enter and sit in a row

All the women other than Lorraine have brought a book of some sort. Liz has her briefcase open and is using an electronic organizer, making it clear that she's not interested in communicating

Caro (*to Helen*) We didn't plan it... Chris had suddenly got very Catholic and wanted everything to be—you know—natural between us. His family is Irish. Well... Anglo-Irish, but his mother's still very, you know, churchified. We knew there was a chance I'd get pregnant, of course, but it was what we both wanted, so... (*She smiles happily*)

Helen nods/smiles politely and gets on with reading her book

Is this your first?
Helen Yes. (*She can't resist*) I've come to it rather late, haven't I?
Caro Oh, I didn't mean it like that—sorry—I just meant... (*She does a vague gesture of "isn't it all exciting"*)
Helen We've both been married before. Don has two teenage children. My first husband died, oh, just six months after we were married. It seemed so unfair, he was ... anyway, it was a long time before I could even look at another man. The thought of re-marrying never entered my head—and as for children ... well, it all seemed much too late for that. And then ... along came Don. (*She smiles*)

Caro returns the smile and Helen goes back to her book as Jan and Patrick "communicate" with Vicki, who will look from one to the other, almost with her mouth open

Jan I've been with Patrick since I was seventeen and he was twenty-four. He taught me everything. About sex ... and politics ... and lentils. Everything, really.
Patrick But quite frankly, after nearly eight years together, we were both becoming aware that Jan was in danger of out-growing our relationship.
Jan As far as *we* were concerned—Patrick and me.
Patrick The thrill had gone.
Jan We discussed it.
Patrick As we discuss everything.
Jan So it was very much a joint decision.
Patrick And decided we needed...
Jan ...A child.
Patrick Preferably a Pisces.
Jan Having a baby will be...
Patrick & Jan ...A manifestation of our love.

Vicki remains staring at them for a moment and then snaps into:

Act I

Vicki I'm so regular it's ridiculous. Miss an *hour* and I know I've clicked, I'm one of them, you know what I mean? And I click so *easy*. I mean you take our Jeremy. I was pregnant with him the minute we got married. Well ... give or take five minutes to get to the hotel.

Now it's Jan's and Patrick's turn to stare

Lorraine (*to no-one in particular*) I'm dying for a wee.

The other women react variously

   (*To Liz*) You mustn't, though, must you?
Liz No. (*She pointedly goes back to her book*)

Slight pause

Lorraine They have to test it to see if you've got diabetes or anything.

Liz almost corrects her, but instead just nods and smiles, a little embarrassed at being involved in Lorraine's naïvety

Lorraine It's funny how they can tell, though, really, isn't it?
Liz Sorry?
Lorraine How they can tell. That you're pregnant. From your wee.
Liz Yes. (*She goes back to her book*)

Pause

Patrick Excuse me...

They all look at him

   When you conceive, a hormone called human chorionic gonadotrophin hCG is released into the bloodstream soon after the embryo has embedded in the uterus. The test shows up the hCG in the urine.
Lorraine Yes, I suppose it would, really.

Pause

Jan D'you know, Patrick, I'm really thirsty.
Patrick I'll fetch you some tea.
Vicki Down the corridor, just past the bookshop.
Patrick Thank you. Would you fancy a cup of dandelion and stinging nettle?
Vicki I think they only do bricklayer's.

Patrick holds up a sachet

Jan We always bring our own.
Patrick Ordinary tea reduces the absorption of iron and should therefore be avoided.
Vicki No, thanks all the same.

Patrick makes to go

Patrick (*confidentially, to Vicki*) They think Jesus was a Pisces.
Vicki Get away.

Patrick exits

Pause

Caro (*generally, happily*) If someone had told me a year ago that not only was I going to have a baby but that I'd want to have it, I would have said...
Liz ...are you out of your mind? Listen—if I'd wanted a kid I wouldn't have just forked out for a one bedroom flat. A kid—are you kidding?
Lorraine It's all I've ever wanted, a baby of my own.
Helen I'm thirty-nine years old. All right, forty. I really had come to the conclusion that babies were things that happen to other people.
Vicki So I goes round to see my mum and I says "I've only gone and done it again" I says and she says "oh gawd not again" and I says "I've just said that" and she says "yes and you said it last time an' all".
Jan ...we really hadn't thought about it—I mean not until we'd made up our minds to have one. But when I knew—I was just so happy.
All (*with varying degrees of enthusiasm*) Join the club.
Liz It was a mistake. End of story.
Lorraine ...the thing is... you're not really a woman till you've had a baby, are you?

The others turn to look at her

Jan It's what you might call the natural course of events.

The others turn to look at her

Don't you think...?

Song 3: In the Club
It's like the moment you know
Like the second it starts

Act I

	Like when the seed starts to grow
Liz	You're breaking our hearts
Jan	Like the moment you miss
Vicki	Is she always like this?
Jan	Like you feel strangely lyrical
	Well why not? It's a miracle
All	So they say

Caro	You know the wondrous thing is
	In a moment supreme
	A baby that's his
	It's all gone like a dream
	One short year to the day
	Since he happened my way
	And I'm unshakably
	Quite unmistakably…
All	In the club!

Liz You want the truth? I hate children. I hate babies. I hate everything to do with them. I don't know anyone who's got one and as far as I'm concerned…

Lorraine …I mean you work until you get married and then you stop and have babies.

Helen If I'm honest—I mean *really* honest… (*But she can't bring herself to say it and shakes her head*)

Jan …it's the link between the past and the future.

Liz Some future.

Vicki	So I says "Mum, it's OK
	You know I've had one before"
	And she says "that's what you'll say
	When you've had twenty-four"
	I says "I'm way overdue
	And I still ain't told Stu"
	She says "Vicki, he's your hubby"
	"That's right" I says, "he got me
	In the club!"

Helen	It was a soft moonlit night
	In Corfu, I recall
	But no—it's not right
	Shouldn't be here at all
	It's all much too late
Lorraine	So surely it's fate?
Helen	Yes, I'll be adventurous

There can't be many pensioners
In the club
Vicki ...Are you going to have it, she says...
Jan ...at least nowadays we've got the choice.
Liz You reckon?
Jan I mean not like in our mothers' day when...
Helen ...romance I suppose you'd call it.
Lorraine All I've wanted to be
Ever since I was small
Is (*speaking*) married, you see,
To someone like my Paul
I'm so glad that I did
Liz Christ, she's only a kid
Lorraine I want to start a family
I know this is right for me
Right for me

Liz So what's so profound
About getting banged up?
The world spins around
And still we end up
Out here on this ledge
This thick end of the wedge
So be realistic
You're one more statistic
In the club!
Caro Well, if that's the way you feel...
Liz Yes?
Lorraine You could...
Liz Yes?
Helen You could...
Liz No! Now I'm here, here I stay.
Vicki For nine months anyway...
All In the club

Yes we're all on our way
All starting to grow
All feeling *au fait*
With those things we should know
'bout this journey ahead
And those thoughts left unsaid
'bout what's growing inside of me
This life that is trying to be

Act I

>But will it come with guarantee
>This bouncing baby on my knee
>It's time for us to think of me
>It's time for us to make our plea
>For us, all us girls
>In the club

The music ends

Don enters. He is dressed as a doctor

Don (*as Doctor*) Sorry to keep you waiting, ladies—have you all filled in your forms?

In unison, each woman raises a form and lets it concertina-open to four pages containing dozens of questions and answers

Any problems?

Lorraine half-raises a hand but decides against it

Jolly good.

A buzzer sounds and a red light flashes

Ah! This way, please.

The women will exit as the Doctor calls out their names from his checklist

Mrs Hale… Mrs Ford… Mrs Masters… Mrs Beckett… Mrs Cope … and Mrs Spencer.
Liz Mss!

Patrick enters with his polystyrene cup of herbal tea

He is somewhat surprised to find the women all gone … but sees the Doctor and moves quickly to him

The busy Doctor exits during the following

Patrick Ah—Doctor—one or two "DOs and DON'Ts" I'd like to run past you if I may… (*He puts the cup on the doctor's clipboard and refers to a sheet of paper*) One, we want an upright delivery, preferably under water

... two, we don't want the baby delivered by someone we've never met ... three, we want the birth to be as natural as possible, we don't want any of these white gowns and masks ... four... (*He glances up to see that the Doctor has already gone. He makes to go after him*)

Jan enters

How did you get on?

She plonks herself down and he will sit next to her

Jan Honestly, doctors. I said to him... I've been here for three and a half hours since which time I've been poked, prodded, pushed around, examined and discussed and what seems to matter least of all is *me*. And when I mentioned The Radical Midwives Association, he practically laughed in my face. Or he would have done, if he hadn't been ... you know. Honestly—how could someone so unperceptive call himself a doctor?
Patrick We'll find someone else. Someone to suit us.
Jan Honestly, he made me so *angry*.

He indicates for her to calm herself and get into the meditative mood... which she does, so that they both have their eyes closed

Patrick Of course you're angry ... you're concerned for the welfare of your child ... make a truce with your feelings: focus on the positive. Let all the negatives go.
Jan Well I shall certainly let *him* go.

The doctor enters busily, still with the cup on his clipboard. He is about to exit but sees Patrick and Jan. He puts the cup into Patrick's left hand and exits

Patrick's eyes open ... he sees the cup and goes after the doctor

Patrick Excuse me, Doctor ... excuse me, excuse me.

Patrick exits

Jan opens her eyes in time to see him go

Jan Patrick... Patrick... Patrick!

Jan exits hurriedly after them

Act I

Chris and Caro enter. Caro is holding a new maternity dress against her body

Caro (*of the new dress*) There.
Chris You certainly didn't waste any time.
Caro I went straight from the hospital. You do realize I'm going to fill this thing?
Chris You'll look terrific.

They embrace, but we can see from his face that he has other thoughts on his mind as they remain in the embrace

Caro I intend being the perfect mother.

Pause

Chris Yes. (*He kisses her briefly and then, still in the embrace, but not looking directly at her*) Caro... I think we should get married.

Pause

Caro But I thought we said...
Chris (*breaking away from her*) ...Yes, we did. But now I think we should get married.
Caro Not ... your mother thinks we should...
Chris ...No, *I* think ... all right, she's—made noises—but... I really think it would be—the right thing. Not just for us ... for the child.

Pause. She knows just what a great influence his parents have on Chris, but she isn't prepared to pursue it

Caro Are you asking me to marry you?

He gets down on one knee

Chris I'm asking you to marry me.

He reaches up to take her hands and she kneels to face him

Caro Not just because I'm heavy with child.
Chris Partly—but mostly because you're very very rich. Well?

Pause. Then, she kisses him

We see Vicki sitting, replacing the plug on an electric iron. She is humming quietly to herself

Stuart enters, wiping his hands on a small towel

Vicki glances up

Vicki (*not heavily*) I thought you were doing some over-time tonight. (*She carries on fixing the plug*)
Stuart He wanted me to fix his bike.
Vicki Better get your skates on, hadn't you? (*She resumes her humming*)
Stuart I said half seven. (*He stands by the door, watching her, smiling fondly*)

She looks up

Vicki (*again, not heavily*) What are you laughing at?
Stuart (*moving in*) Not laughing. Smiling. Thinking.
Vicki Oh yeah? What about?

She puts the iron down on the floor next to her as he moves to stand behind her

Song 4: Would You Miss Me
Stuart   'bout... lots of things
    'bout... you and me
    'bout... how we met
    'bout stuff like that
Vicki   'bout time you went (*She looks at him directly*)
    Isn't it?

But she doesn't resist as he briefly kisses the top of her head and moves to sit beside her, putting his arm around her, and gently setting her head against his shoulder

Stuart   Been thinking about things a lot today
Vicki   Been thinking about things what today?

Stuart   Oh...
    Thinking that I want to get home
    Be here with you and the kids
    Knowing for me that's where it's at
Vicki   Go on, Mister

Act I

	Off you go
	Do some work
	Earn some dough
Stuart	I love you
Vicki	Yes I know (*She makes to move*)
	Off you go
Stuart	No, don't go away
	Just… stay as you are
	Resting your head
Vicki	You're supposed to be working (*Her head remains on his shoulder*)
	Earning us bread
Stuart	Yeah yeah, I'm going
Vicki	Yeah yeah, you said
Stuart	Give us a kiss
Vicki	You never miss (*She kisses his cheek briefly*)
	Do you?
Stuart	Would you miss me?

She puts her head back on his shoulder and he takes her hand

Vicki When?
Stuart   If ever I went
Vicki Where?
Stuart   Off with some chick
Vicki   Sounds heavensent
Stuart   These things occur
Vicki   Good luck to her
             And would I miss what?
             What have you got?
Stuart   Got a van
Vicki   'bout the lot
Stuart   Got some great leather strides
Vicki   And what else besides?
Stuart   Got a heart full of love
Vicki   Full of chat, give you that
Stuart   Say you love me
Vicki On your way. (*Thumbs towards the door*)
Stuart Say it—just once.
Vicki   Love you—OK?
Stuart Give us a kiss then
Vicki   Last one today (*She kisses his cheek*)
  Maybe.

They smile gently at each other ... then sit a moment ... and then, as though moved by some sudden disturbing thought, he briefly kisses her cheek and gets up and moves away

Vicki You all right?

He attempts a reassuring smile

Stuart I've had some funny old thoughts today. Strange what comes into your head, isn't it? You're driving along and suddenly... (*And again the little smile—but he remains with his back to her*) See...
        Sometimes I feel...
Vicki What?
Stuart   Frightened, I guess
Vicki Of what?
Stuart   Of what I've got
Vicki (*shrugging*) Others got less
Stuart   No, I don't mean that
           That's not what I meant
           I mean...
           God, how I love you
           God, if you went...

Pause. The intensity of his feelings has moved her but, unable to respond, she makes light of it, as always

Vicki   You're a dope
Stuart Yeah.
Vicki   Really are
Stuart Yeah.
Vicki   Always were
Stuart Yeah.
Vicki   Go too far
            Go to work
Stuart   Give us a kiss then

He kisses her brow

Vicki   Where would I go
            Anyway? (*She looks at him*)

They smile at each other and she reaches up to take his hand and he kisses her briefly and remains holding her hand

Act I

Stuart Give 'em a kiss for me
Vicki Course.
Stuart Tell 'em goodnight
Vicki I will.
Stuart Tell 'em a story
Vicki Yeah, yeah, all right.
Stuart 'Bout how their father
Who was really a frog (*He briefly kisses her hand and moves to the door*)
Vicki True.
Stuart Met this princess
Vicki Yeah, (*singing*) who fancied a snog.
Stuart 'Bout how he drank
From her beautiful lips
Vicki Oh, *please*.
Stuart 'Bout how she makes him
Vicki Yes?
Stuart A great egg and chips
Vicki Yeah, that's about the size of it.
Stuart But mostly how he loves her
Vicki You're gonna be late.
Stuart How he really loves her (*at the door*)
Vicki You're hopeless.
Stuart Loves her
Vicki Off!
Stuart Loves her

Stuart goes

Pause

Vicki And how if she could say
If she could find the way
To tell him...

Pause. She resumes humming rather than finish the thought

(*More to herself*) Love you?...Course I love you ... go on, Mister ... go to work.

She continues ironing and humming and the music finishes

Note: from now until the end of Act I, the women will each exhibit a four-month bulge

Lorraine enters, looking a little tired and breathless, carrying a small bag of shopping

She sits, grateful to take the weight off her feet, eases off her shoes. She closes her eyes

Almost immediately, Paul's head appears round a corner

Paul (*calling*) Lolly?
Lorraine (*calling back*) In here. (*She quickly puts her shoes back on*)
Paul Close your eyes, I've got a surprise.
Lorraine What is it?
Paul A surprise. Are they closed?
Lorraine (*eyes closed*) Yes.
Paul Promise?
Lorraine Promise.

Paul disappears ... then he enters, carrying a huge—and rather cheap—teddy bear

He crosses and holds the bear before her

Paul Da-da!

She opens her eyes

Lorraine Oh Paul, it's lovely.
Paul D'you like it?
Lorraine It's lovely. (*But*) It must have cost a fortune.
Paul No— (*he kisses her*) this bloke I know.
Lorraine Yes but... (*She changes her mind and reaches up to take the bear and cuddles it to her*) You are, Mister Ted, you're really lovely.

Paul smiles down at them

Paul (*suddenly remembering*) How did it go at the hospital?
Lorraine Oh ... they did tests and everything—you know.
Paul And everything's all right?
Lorraine Course it is. (*She reaches out a hand for his as though for reassurance*) I'll get your tea.
Paul No, no, you sit there, I'll do it... (*He indicates the shopping*) This it, is it?

She nods, smiling, and he takes up the bag and moves away

Act I

You are all right, are you?
Lorraine Bit tired, that's all...
Paul ...should've let *me* do the shopping...
Lorraine ...don't be soppy...
Paul ...we're gonna have to move, Lolly...
Lorraine ...no...
Paul ...another month and them stairs'll be impossible...
Lorraine ...it'll be all right...
Paul ...we'll need another room anyway...
Lorraine ...Paul—we can't afford to move... we can only afford this place because I'm working... I mean I'm not complaining but... it'll be all right. Honest.

Pause

Paul Yeah. Well. I've got a few ideas, so we'll see. (*Again he kisses her briefly and makes to go*)
Lorraine Paul... It's twins. I saw them on the scan. We're having twins.

Pause. He stands looking at her as she sits, clutching the bear

Liz enters, using the cordless telephone and carrying a glass. She will sit and pour herself a glass of red wine during the following

Liz Yes! Then he asks me if I've got any problems. How do I know, I said, I'm pregnant, how do I know if the way I feel is a problem or if it's normal? Normal when you're pregnant, I mean... I'd shoot myself if I thought this was *normal* normal... as long as I can think of it as abnormal, I can cope. Christ, how do people have *two* babies? (*She sits*) Listen—Sally—if you're not busy, why don't you come round, I've just opened a bottle of wine... no, I know I'm not supposed to, I just lick the label but that wouldn't... ah, right, when's he due back? Right. Some other time then. (*With an edge*) No, I'm not lonely, I just thought it would be nice to ... what? No, I haven't heard from him, I don't expect to and yes, I'm coping very well, thank you. Yeah ... yeah, that would be good. Yeah. Bye, Sal. (*After a pause, sardonically*) Am I coping? (*She tosses the phone into the chair*)

Song 5: I Don't Need It

(*Speaking*) That's rich!
        Patronising bitch!
        What does she think I am?
        Well, sorry to tell you

My "dear old friend"
It might be a shock
But it isn't the end
You'll have to go elsewhere
To condescend
I don't need it
Comprehend?
Don't need it

They're all the same
With their phoney concern
Well, it's true what they say
We live and we learn
So start learning, friends
The lady's not for turning, friends
She just needs more discerning friends
Who keep shtum
Give me room
I don't need it!

And I don't need him
Don't need his "support"
Want to know what I think?
I don't give him a thought
I made it clear
That I was not persuaded, dear
So why should we evade it, dear
He's gone
And for one
I don't need him
Shown his heels
Cut the spiel
So who needs him?

Friends!
Sanctimonious friends!
What do they think I am?
OK, you're right
I can't deny
It's a mistake
I could rectify
But plucky old me
I'm getting by

Act I

>Which, believe me, I know
>Is one in the eye
>For you and him
>And all the rest
>And I refuse to be
>Down or depressed
>In fact I'm remarkably
>Self-possessed
>There, aren't you impressed
>I don't need it!
>
>So cross my heart
>And hope to die
>I've made my bed
>And I'm happy to lie...
>I'm not lying, pals
>Just listen, my old trying pals
>My faithful, faithless, undying pals
>We're fine
>Me and mine
>We don't need it
>Don't phone
>Leave me alone
>Don't need it

Pause. Then she takes up a book boldly entitled How To Stop Smoking *and sits reading*

Lorraine enters

We are in the ante-natal clinic

Lorraine (*sitting next to Liz*) Hallo.
Liz (*looking up from her book*) Oh. Hallo. (*She goes back to her book*)

Slight pause

Lorraine I've got to have another scan today. Have you had yours yet?
Liz (*not looking up*) Yes.
Lorraine Could you see anything?
Liz Not much, no.
Lorraine It's fantastic really, isn't it? I mean, could you tell if it was a boy or a...

Liz ...I don't want to know.
Lorraine No. Neither do I.

Caro enters, wearing her maternity dress

Caro (*bright and friendly*) Hallo.

Liz gives her a cursory smile and goes back to her book. Lorraine's smile is friendly. Caro sits next to her

Shouldn't be so bad this time. Not so much hanging about.
Lorraine I wish my husband could be here. All these questions they ask you. I say yes to everything. You do, though, don't you?

Liz looks up from her book as Patrick, Vicki and Jan enter and will sit during the following

Patrick (*to Vicki*) We meditate twice daily—for peace of mind.
Vicki (*fascinated by Patrick and Jan*) Oh—yeah—right.
Jan A poor mental condition means a poor physical condition.
Vicki Right.
Patrick Jan is prone to nervous sensitivity.
Vicki Yeah?
Jan I worry about things, it's so stupid.
Vicki Yeah—right.
Patrick What we try to do is minimize those worries, put them in perspective.
Jan I have limitations on what I can cope with, you see.
Vicki My sister's like that. She has trouble with her internals and the doctor said she'd better have it done so she says "are you saying I've got to have an eastereggtomy" and he says "a what?" and she says "an ex-directory" and he says "*hysterectomy*" and she says "well, whatever you call it, the point is will it affect my sex life?" and he said "oh, no, my dear, we'll be taking away the baby carriage, but we'll be leaving you the playpen". Saucy bugger.
Lorraine (*to Caro*) I feel so tired all the time so I force down food to give myself some energy and somehow it only makes it worse.
Caro The thing to do, surely, is to try to organise one's fatigue—take regular little naps and so on.
Liz (*lowering her book*) Not so easy, though, is it, if one has a job to do. (*She goes back to her book*)

We should sense that she has chipped in to protect Lorraine

Act I

Caro Oh God, sorry, that did sound awfully smug, didn't it?
Lorraine (*smiling*) Just a bit.
Caro Sorry.
Jan I think it's awful, spending all that money on maternity clothing you'll hate to wear and then throw away—well, give away.
Vicki *Right.*
Patrick Not that we intend buying special clothing.
Jan No, I mean the principle ... the pressures on people ... buy buy buy.
Vicki *Right.*
Patrick It's all down to improvisation, really.
Vicki *Right.*
Liz Maternity wear was designed by some sadistic little nun to punish you for having sex in the first place.
Lorraine Actually ... they've got some very nice things in British Home Stores.
Helen (*off*) Thank you.

Helen enters, R. *She looks concerned*

Vicki (*to Helen*) You all right, love?
Helen (*emotionally*) Sorry? Oh—yes I'm fine—thanks. I've just had the results of my—you know, the test—and everything's in the clear, so I'm—well, you can imagine, it's been—you know—it's been something of a worry.

Vicki moves quickly to her

Vicki Course it has, love—here, where's that nurse, that wassername, Harpoon Annie—see if she can't rustle you up a cuppa tea.
Helen No, I'm fine, thanks—really—I would like to telephone my husband, though—you don't know if there's a...
Vicki (*indicating* US) ...Down the corridor on the right.
Helen Thanks.

During the following, Vicki and Helen move US, *as Vicki shows Helen the way and Helen exits*

Lorraine (*to Jan*) Are you only having the one, then?
Jan Sorry?
Lorraine The way you was talking... I wondered whether you was planning to have just the one baby.
Caro I'm sure I shall have lots. I feel like a convert to a new religion.

Vicki moves back DS

Lorraine (*to Vicki*) Was your baby planned?
Vicki No, I got knocked up, didn't I? Same as I did with my Jeremy and my Samantha. I know exactly when it was, mind—it was coming home in the van from his brother's birthday party. They had a lotta that Spanish champagne which is fatal because my trouble is, I cannot resist a sexual overture especially if it's in a lay-by off the A11. He says I am what is known as a Legover In My Own Lifetime.

All eyes are on her now—and she is enjoying winding them up

Jan Who says, umm…?
Vicki Him. My bloke. Stuart.
Liz Can't you … take precautions?
Vicki Pardon?
Patrick Can't you practise birth control?
Vicki We do. We practise the Pentonville Method.

Pause. No-one likes to ask what that method is

Jan The, umm… Pentonville Method?
Vicki It's all to do with the timing. Every time he comes out of Pentonville I fall for a baby.

They all look at her, none of them sure how to take her

Patrick (*to Jan*) I'll just see if I can find that doctor. (*Generally*) I just want to run through the Le Boyer method with him.

Patrick exits, passing Helen entering

Helen What I love is how women you've never met before can't resist telling you how *their* pregnancy went.
Vicki And it's always a horror story…

Music - start of Oh The Pain

"How I Gave Birth And Just About Lived To Tell The Tale".

The others ad lib their agreement and will assume "women's voices" during the following

Vicki I went in fourteen stone and I came out six.
Liz I have what is known as a contracted pelvis.

Act I   33

Jan Yes, I had two of those.
Helen I were that big, I were like an elephant.

They all suck in air in dramatic unison

Song 6: Oh The Pain

Helen	I began…
Others	She began
Helen	…My contractions
Others	Whoo
Helen	At twenty past nine
Others	Oah
Helen	The doctor said wonderful!
	You're doing fine!
	Three days go by
	And still there's no sign
	Just the pain!
Others	Ooh
Helen	Constant pain!
Others	Ooh
Helen	But still I'd go through it again!

Liz Well.
            I went
Others   Went?
Liz Into labour
Others Ooh
Liz At quarter to five
Others   And then?
Liz Come noon the next day
            And it's yet to arrive
            They said it's a miracle
            You're still alive.
            And the pain!
All   Oh, the pain!
Liz But still I'd go through it again!

Jan It's like…
Helen   Having your eyeballs
                Filled up with lead
Jan Or…
Liz Having your top lip
            Pulled over your head

Jan Or...
Vicki ...Better for her
If we left it unsaid
Jan & Vicki She'll soon understand
What it is women dread
All Women 'Bout the pain!
God, the pain!
But still we'd go through it again!

Jan The specialist said it's a wonder she's walking, let alone about to give birth.
I hung
Others Hung
Jan On that rack
Others Ooh
Jan Twisted almost in half
Others My God
Jan Crying out for some help
But there wasn't the staff
They were all in the lounge
Watching *Game For A Laugh*
Full of pain!
All Women Wracked with pain!
Jan But still I'd go through it again.

Others Whoo
Vicki It's a funny sort of pain really.
I was in
Others She was in
Vicki Labour
Others Whoo
Vicki For over a week
Others A week
Vicki These students kept popping in
Just for a peek
You feel less like a woman
And more like a freak
Well, it's not very nice, is it?
Not very chic.
All And the pain!
Blinding pain!
But still we'd go through it again!

Helen All this breathing you do's

Act I

                A complete waste of time
                It's a joke, it's a farce,
                A complete pantomime
Liz I lay on that table
                Fighting for life
                There's only one answer, they said
                It's the knife!
Vicki   The hours I suffered
                The hours I waited
                Semi-unconscious
                And fully-dilated
Jan I lay gasping for air
Liz Like a whale on a beach
Jan When they offered me drugs
                I said I'll have one of each
All Women Stop the pain!
                Stop the pain!
Helen & Jan But still we'd go through it
Liz & Vicki Yes, still we'd go through it
All Women Yes still we'd go through it again!

Helen They said.
Others   Push
Helen I said how?
  They said.
Others   Shove!
Helen I said now?
  They said.
Others   Yes!
Helen I said ow!
  They said.
Others   Try!
Helen I said cow!
Others   And the pain!
All Women Endless pain!
                But still—we'd go through it—a—gain!

The music ends and a red light pings on and we hear the tannoy call "Mrs Hale?"

    Jan exits

Caro Will you carry on working after the baby?

Lorraine That's what's worrying me.
Caro There is this belief, isn't there, that the mother should be at home for the first three years or so.
Lorraine It's whether you can afford it, isn't it?

Caro realizes she's on uncomfortable ground here and brightly changes the subject

Caro (*to Vicki*) I hope my baby's not too big.
Vicki Pardon?
Caro I was saying—I'd much prefer a small baby.
Vicki So would I, love—d'you fancy going halves on one?

A light pings on and the tannoy calls "Mrs Beckett"

Caro Miss Beckett, actually... (*Generally, with a happy smile*) Mrs Sullivan next Thursday.

Caro exits

Vicki (*more to herself*) Well, there's a turn-up.
Liz Why do women have to justify having children *and* a job?
Lorraine Being a mum's a job in itself, though, really, isn't it?
Liz Situation vacant... incredibly dull job, eighteen hours a day, seven days a week, twelve months a year, eighteen years if you're lucky, more like twenty-five if you're not ... no holidays, no over-time, a guaranteed reduced standard of living, and no escape.

A light pings on and the tannoy calls "Mrs Cope?"

Vicki (*to Liz*) You *are* having this baby by choice, I take it?

Vicki exits

Pause

Liz Listen—don't take any notice of me, I'm...
Lorraine ...No, that's all right.

Pause

I'm having twins.
Liz Oh. (*She's unsure whether or not congratulations are in order*)

Act I

Lorraine We're really happy about it.
Liz Well that's—good.
Lorraine I mean it was a bit of a shock at first—we had no idea, you see, I mean there's nothing in the family or anything—but we are, we're really happy about it. Mind you, I wish our flat was a bit bigger. It's really small. Too small, really. Paul—my husband—calls it our stone tent. I'm going round the council after, see if we can get moved up but where we live everyone's on the list. Still. You just have to make the best of it, really, don't you?

A moment, and Liz can't resist asking

Liz How old are you?
Lorraine I'm older than I look actually. I'm eighteen.

A light pings on and the tannoy calls "Mrs Ford?" Lorraine makes to exit

Will you be going to the classes?
Liz I'm not sure. I doubt it.
Lorraine My friend says they're really good.
Liz Oh well, in that case...

They exchange little smiles

Lorraine exits

Liz is left alone. The tannoy calls "Mrs Spencer"

Liz moves to exit as Patrick enters, pre-occupied

Liz (*to Patrick*) Mss.

Liz exits

Patrick sits, starts to meditate

Stuart enters

Patrick, still pre-occupied, doesn't acknowledge him. Stuart sits, away from him, takes out a packet of cigarettes and is about to light one when Patrick's eyes open and he gives Stuart a reproving look. Stuart re-pockets the cigarettes

Stuart 'Ow do.

Patrick Morning.

Slight pause

Stuart You a dad?
Patrick (*nodding*) Yes.
Stuart Waiting for the missus?
Patrick Yes.
Stuart Me an' all. (*He vaguely indicates their surroundings*) Right carnival, innit?

Pause. Patrick is unable to resist sharing his news with someone

Patrick Actually, we've just been told that she's got high blood pressure.
Stuart (*nodding, understandingly*) Oh, right—so she'll have to come in for a bit, will she?
Patrick No, we—er—we look after ourselves.
Stuart Oh, yeah?
Patrick We like things to be as natural as possible.
Stuart Oh, yeah?
Patrick Alternative medicine.
Stuart Oh—yeah—plants an' that—right.
Patrick Right.
Stuart (*nodding; suddenly*) Here... (*He moves along to sit next to Patrick*) You might be entitled to Sickness Benefit. She is working is she, your missus?
Patrick Well, for the moment she is, yes.
Stuart So you'll be putting in for SMP.
Patrick Umm...
Stuart Your Statutory Maternity Pay.
Patrick Oh, umm ... we're not actually into that side of things yet...
Stuart ...Oh, yes, you must have your SMP. You work for it, you're entitled, right?
Patrick The thing is, what does it, umm, what does it actually *provide*?
Stuart Well, I haven't actually made a study of it, but I do know a bit. For example... to get it, your SMP, she—your good lady—has to be employed by the same people for at least six months and to be working in the fifteenth week before the baby is due, i.e. when she's twenty-six weeks pregnant— and of course she's had to be earning enough to pay Class One National Insurance Contributions. You're with me so far?
Patrick Umm...
Stuart ...On the other hand, if you can't get your SMP, you might be able to get a weekly maternity allowance from Social Security, but here again

Act I

she'll have had to have paid standard rate Class One or Class Two NI contributions for at least twenty-six weeks during a set period. And of course, if you or your lady are getting income support or family credit, you may be able to get a social fund maternity payment to help with the expenses of which in my experience there are more than a few. On top of that o'course there's your free prescriptions, your dental health, your milk and so forth... (*He glances up, giving a little wave, towards the unseen Vicki*) There she is, my little queen. Now is she or is she not a real looker? I love that woman. I do, I really love her. (*He stands*) The thing to do is pop down to the SS and get yourself a claims form—SF 100—and you might pick up a copy of FB8 while you're about it—Babies And Benefits—see you around, eh—be lucky—and, oh, yeah—don't worry about the blood pressure, they're very good these people ... waddaya think of the name Gervaise?

Patrick Very nice.
Stuart Gervaise ... or Siobhan.

Stuart exits

Patrick sits for a moment and then exits in the opposite direction

We see Helen who sits on the bed, writing a birthday card

Don enters and stands behind her

He kisses her head and puts his hands on her shoulders

Don What's this?

He will gently massage her shoulders and she will continue writing during the following

Helen One of the girls at work. It's her birthday. (*She shows him the card*) What d'you think?
Vicki Very nice. I've booked a table at Lorenzo's.
Helen That's a bit posh.
Don We're celebrating. (*He kisses her head*) Eight o'clock, OK?

She smiles, nods, and he is about to move away but she catches his hand

Helen I've been a real pain, haven't I? You must have wondered what you'd let yourself in for ... especially as good old Wendy seems to have sailed through it twice without so much as creasing her knickers.

Don She happens to have had two very straightforward pregnancies besides which we said we weren't going to talk about her.
Helen Yes. Yes, we did. I'm sorry.

Pause. Then he again kisses her briefly and is about to move away

Helen (*with her back to him*) I just wish… I just wish she wasn't *there* all the time.

Pause. He will move back to her and put his hands on her shoulders during the following

Don (*gently*) I know it drives you crazy but I have to maintain some sort of relationship with her because of the children…
Helen I know… I know…
Don …She's on her own and all right, yes, to some extent that concerns me … you can't live with someone for fourteen years and just … erase them. Well, at least *I* can't. And I know sometimes I don't think and I talk about *her* and what *she* felt when she was pregnant, but it's only because I've been through all this before and I just wanted to convince you that what you're feeling isn't…
Helen I know I know I know—I over-react and I really will try to stop it.
Don We'll *both* try to stop it—OK?

Pause

Helen (*smiling and touching his hand*) OK.

He kisses her gently. The phone rings. They freeze—both knowing who it will be. He gives her a brief kiss and answers the phone. Helen sits, her back to Don as he takes up the receiver, willing it not to be her

Don Hallo? (*He almost closes his eyes in despair*) Oh—yes—hallo, Wendy—well, as a matter of fact we were just going out, but—er—what can I do for you? (*He continues to listen, talk into the phone but we do not hear what he is saying and all the time he is aware of Helen*)
Helen You see? (*She continues to look at him for a moment and then moves to sit* DR, *her back to him*)

Pause

Don Yes, all right, I'll take care of it. (*He replaces the receiver*)

Music

Act I

Song 7: If Only

If only I could find a way
To do what's for the best
If only I knew what to say
To set her mind at rest

If only I could make her see
The past is not a threat
If only she could see in me
That I have no regret

It's only from our own mistakes
We see things as they were
I only know the one mistake
I didn't make was her

To hear her voice, to feel her touch,
To love and not compare
To catch the smile that says so much
Just knowing she is there

The music continues to underscore

I only know she makes me see
The future's ours to live
And only she awakes in me
The love I have to give

If only she could read my mind
Could feel the way I feel
Among the memories left behind
It's only her that's real

Pause

We see Lorraine and Paul. He is holding a set of keys and is excited. She looks around, apprehensive. It's somewhere she hasn't seen before. He will move around, miming opening doors or indicating

Paul Bathroom ... kitchen ... master bedroom—lovely fitted wardrobe, look ... second bedroom—not big, I know, but big enough for...
Lorraine Yes, but what did he say, this man?
Paul He said if I want it, I can have it.

Lorraine Yes, but why, Paul?
Paul What d'you mean "why", Lolly?
Lorraine I mean ... who is he, this man?
Paul This man I know ... he's one of our big customers at the garage and he heard I was looking for somewhere and he said have a look at this place.
Lorraine Yes, but... (*she wants to persist in her line of questioning about "this man", but changes it to*) can we afford it, Paul? I mean we'd have to buy furniture and everything and...
Paul Just say you like it ... that's all ... just say you like it.

Pause. She moves to him, embraces him

Lorraine I think it's lovely.
Paul You see, I want to give you the best...
Lorraine I know... I know...

This moment between them, her arms about him

Paul I'll tell him we'll think about it, then, shall I?
Lorraine Yes. Tell him we'll think about it.

And they remain together

> *Stuart enters, dressed as a four star hotel porter, carrying an expensive suitcase which he puts down*

> *Chris enters, carrying Caro. Both are wearing their wedding suits and flower buttonholes. Each holds a glass of champagne, he holds a champagne bottle. So that it is a giggly, rather inelegant entrance*

Chris (*of the room*) All right?
Caro Perfect.

He carries her across to look out of the window

Chris And there you have your English Channel.
Caro What, that grey thing?
Stuart That's the one.

> *Stuart exits*

Chris and Caro kiss, then he lets her down and refills their glasses

Chris To us.

Act I

Caro The three of us.
Chris (*with a slight edge*) Oh yes ... mustn't forget ... the three of us.

They drink. She catches sight of herself in a mirror and moves to stand before it, turning sideways so that we get the full benefit of her very obvious bulge

Caro D'you think he noticed?
Chris Who?
Caro The registrar.
Chris Let's have a look.

She deliberately makes the bulge look bulgier

Possibly. (*He refills their glasses*) I'm sorry my parents couldn't be there.
Caro It doesn't matter.
Chris To hell with 'em—right?
Caro Right.

Pause. He kisses her

Chris Well, then, Mrs Sullivan.
Caro Well, then.

Pause

Song 8: Look at Me

Caro	Look at me
	I've never felt like this before
	I've got all I need
	And I have never wanted more
Chris	They've had their say
	I've had my fill
	I love you now
	And always will
Caro	But this could make a difference
	Things can never be the same
Chris	It'll work out right
	I'll always love you
	You understand
Chris & Caro	I'll always love you
	Whatever happens
	That can never change
	This love affair

>   This life we share
>   Was always meant to be
>   Look at us
>   Look at you
>   Look at me

They embrace

> *We hear the sound of humming ... and then we see Jan and Patrick, eyes closed, meditating*

Jan I shall have to give up work until this blood pressure business is sorted out, I suppose.
Patrick I'll take a few days off.
Jan Why?
Patrick To look after you.
Jan I'll be all right.
Patrick No—I want to look after you. Both of you.

She smiles and reaches out a hand towards him. He senses it, and reaches out and they hold hands. They remain like this, hands holding, eyes closed. And we hold this moment of togetherness

Jan (*fondly*) Patrick.
Patrick Mmmm?
Jan (*fondly*) What are you thinking?
Patrick I'm thinking... I'm thinking that what I should do is go along to the DHSS and pick up a copy of FB8.

Slight pause

Jan Copy of what, sorry?
Patrick Sorry—FB8. Babies And Benefits.

Slight pause

Jan Oh.

And they remain thus

> *We see Stuart and Vicki. She is painting a small stool blue. It was pink. He is knitting*

Stuart You what? You told 'em I've done time in Pentonville?

Act I

Vicki I think it's all part of my condition.
Stuart Telling porkies?
Vicki These fantasies I have.
Stuart Well, you coulda said Dartmoor and given me a *bitta* credibility. (*Of the knitting—he's dropped a stitch*) Now look what you've made me do, Victoria: I'm all upset.
Vicki I think it was with that Pauline coming into the shop today.
Stuart Pauline What's-it?
Vicki Yeah.
Stuart You haven't seen her for yonks.
Vicki No.
Stuart He still inside, is he?
Vicki Another six months. That's what must have put the idea into my head.
Stuart (*giving a little jerk of the head*) How is she?
Vicki She's put on four stone and become a Buddhist.
Stuart He won't like that.
Vicki It quite suits her, as it happens.
Stuart What, fat and peaceful.
Vicki That orange colour. I tell you what, though: I'd rather be in prison than on a bus in Karachi.
Stuart What's that got to do with it?
Vicki No, what I'm saying is … just a minute.
Men (*concerned*) What?

And the following comes fast, overlapping almost … as with a gradually escalating mixture of wonderment and apprehension and, in some cases, fear almost

Music and we see all the others

Caro Come here…
Lorraine Feel…
Jan Here…
Helen Give me your hand…
Patrick (*concerned*) Why, what's…
Women Except Liz (*fingers to lips*) Ssshh…
Lorraine (*almost a whisper*) Wait…
Helen Wait.
Women Except Liz There.
Some Women Yes?
Other Women Yes?
Men (*mixed emotions*) Yes.

Patrick My God, it's like...
Paul It feels like...
Jan A butterfly.
Don Yes.
Lorraine A small bird trying to...
Vicki Remember the first time we...
Stuart (*smiling gently*) Yes.
Patrick Yes!
Some Men It's fantastic!
Some Women It's incredible!
Women Except Liz It's our baby.
All (*in unison*) And it's moving!

Lights down, focusing on Liz who is alone

Song 9: I Can Feel It

Liz Can't explain it
Didn't want it
Can't believe it
This feeling I'm feeling
Is hard to believe
But I feel it
Feel it moving
It's so moving
Can't describe it
But I feel it
It's mine

Lights slowly up on the others who are in couples. The women place the men's hands on their bulges, men behind women and all facing DS

Women	You can sense it
	Almost touch it
	You can hold it
	In your hands is our future
	The life we conceived
Men	I can feel it
	Feel it moving
Women	It's your baby
Men	And I love it
Couples	It's yours
	And it's mine...

Music goes into faster tempo

Act I

Women	It's time for us
	To think ahead
	It's now we should
	Prepare the way
	A child that must
	Be clothed and fed
	It won't be long
	Before the day
Men	Things are changing
	And forever
	No more us
	That used to be
All	What will be
	Really has to be
Men	Rearranging
	Whatsoever
	Round this life
	About to be
	I feel it
	It's moving
	My life's
	Got to change
	A feeling
	So moving
	A feeling
	So strange

Women	Now I know it
	I'm a mother
	Won't forget
	Just how I feel
	Crazy feeling
	Oh, so real
	Never thought I'd
	Feel so different
	Never thought I'd
	Be this way
	Couldn't hope for
	Such a day

Men	Can't explain it
	Won't forget it
	Can't believe it
	No point in concealing
	The way that I feel
	It's enthralling
	It's exciting
	It's so moving
	Can't describe it
	This child
	Will be mine

Liz	Who'd have thought it?
	Here I am
	Tough old Liz
	Archetypal Ms
	About to be a mum

Women	You can sense it		
	Almost touch it		
	You can hold it	**Men**	It won't be long
	My head is still reeling		Before it's here
	It's hard to believe		So much to do
	But I feel it		So little time
	Feel it moving		It's yours
	It's our baby		And it's mine
	And I love it		
	It's yours		
	And it's mine		

Men   And then we have to
Choose a name
Rebecca, Kate
Or Tracey
Paul Or Alice.
Chris Or Daisy.
Men   There's David, Simon
Matthew, Sam
A list so long it
Drives you crazy

Women   And don't forget
We must design
And decorate
The baby room
All   Very soon
Paint the baby room
Women   There's things to get
This child of mine
A christening robe
A silver spoon

	I feel it	**Men**	Making plans
	It's moving		And washing pans
	Our life's		And buying prams
	Got to change		A baby chair
	A feeling		Shopping round at
	So moving		Mothercare
	A feeling		Building cots
	So strange		For tiny tots
	A feeling		And buying pots
	So strange		For them to pee

Act I

                                    Blue or pink
                                    For he or she
                                    For he or she

Women   Can't explain it
            Won't forget it
            Can't believe it
            This feeling I'm
              feeling
Men   Can't explain it   **Women**   Is hard to believe
            Won't forget it   But I feel it
            Can't believe it   Feel it moving
            This feeling I'm   It's so moving
              feeling   Can't describe it
            Is hard to believe   But it's real and
            But now we're here
            I understand
            It's real and

All I feel it. (*Ad lib—as opening*) It's moving!

CURTAIN

ACT II

Music

Voice (*off*) Pregnancy is both strenuous and demanding. Gentle exercise will help your body cope with the continuous physiological as well as psychological changes that will occur. Never exercise on a full stomach.

The women and Patrick enter, as a chorus line, each with a top hat and cane. The women, wearing maternity dungarees in bright colours, are now six months pregnant and have bulges of varying sizes. For example, Lorraine's, Vicki's and Liz's will be quite small, while Jan and Helen are rather big. Patrick is wearing a "sympathy" pregnancy pack

During the following, they will dance, expressionless, aware of their physical state

              Song 10: Ladies in Waiting
Women   One by one the ladies in waiting
           Six months gone and three more to go
           Exercise improves circulation
           As we try our bit for the nation
           No pain, no gain

           When we move it's almost perfection
           In the groove, we float like a cloud
           Here's a tip we'd quite like to mention
           Get a grip on pre-natal tension
           It can be such

           Fun to be the ladies in waiting
           Must agree it's doing the trick
           Won't seize up while everything's moving
           This knees-up is our way of proving
           Must be doing

Tap break

           (*Sotto voce*) Good for us, the ladies in…

Act II

Liz Hallo, folks, just look at me now
   The shape of a lemon, the size of a cow
Women   (*sotto voce*) Waiting here till it comes along
Helen Isn't this fun, isn't it jolly
   Another few weeks I'll be needing a trolley
Women   (*sotto voce*) Thought we'd find a nice little night spot
            To impress the world with our foxtrot
            Time to dream once

            More, five, six, the ladies are…
Vicki I used to win prizes down at the palais.
   Last week I was third in a steam engine rally
Women   (*sotto voce*) Waiting here till it comes along
Caro I find it all incredibly super
   But then I would—I'm with BUPA
Women   There you go
            It's super duper

            So high class the ladies in waiting
            Tits and ass and bulges "en suite"
            Everything is coming up roses
            Size D cups and surgical hoses

            Altogether

            In our prime the ladies in waiting
            Three months time the stars of the show
            Stepping out like Liza Minnelli
            Just watch out for us on the telly
Some   Liking it
Others Lumping it
All   Bumping and grinding away, everyday
            The ladies are waiting their day

            Ole!

The music ends

   Everyone except Liz and Lorraine exits

Liz and Lorraine change their shoes etc. … as though at the end of an exercise class. Liz is partway through one of her diatribes

Liz And it's the women who are the worst… I get women I don't even know coming up to me and saying "aren't you absolutely thrilled" and I say "as it happens, no, I'm not, this lump you're salivating over is nothing more than a temporary gap in a very promising career". And that's another thing ... the way my so-called male colleagues see me in a totally different light—suddenly I'm one of "them". They even show me pictures of their grizzly kids. (*She shudders at the thought*) Ugh...

It's all been for her own benefit ... this stoking of the rage that so often seems to burn inside her... Lorraine is just there to rub against. But now Liz becomes aware of Lorraine and smiles and shrugs as if to say "listen to me"

Any luck with the council? About the flat.
Lorraine Oh... (*she smiles*) ...not really, no, not yet. We did look at a place, someone Paul knows, but nothing came of it. I mean it was far too expensive anyway. We could never have afforded it. But Paul has these ideas. He's a bit of a dreamer, my Paul.

There is nothing self-pitying about her: to her, that's the way life is

Liz Don't you have any family that might be able to help?
Lorraine Not really. Paul hasn't got any family—well, his sister, but she's younger than he is. His dad went off when they were just babies and his mum ... well, she went a bit funny and they were brought up by his Auntie Beryl, well, she's not really his auntie, but you know, and she's just got this tiny little place in Camberwell.
Liz What about *your* family?
Lorraine They don't speak to us ... not since me and Paul—you know. It's my dad, really, he's—you know—he's very old-fashioned, my dad. (*She allows herself a rueful little smile*) Still ... they'll come round, I expect—these things always sort themselves out in the end, don't they? It's funny, though, isn't it ... there's me and Paul clicking straight away and there's other couples keep trying for years.
Liz Yes, it's funny all right. Twenty years ago all the medical profession could think about was finding ways of having sex without having babies ... now they spend most of their time trying to find ways of making babies for people who can't make them themselves.

Lorraine smiles ... and Liz actually finds herself smiling back

Lorraine I wish... (*She trails off*)
Liz Wish what?
Lorraine (*shaking her head, smiling*) Don't matter—I'll miss my bus—see you next week, then, shall I... (*She starts to move away*)

Act II

Liz Which way do you go?
Lorraine Acton.
Liz I'll give you a lift.
Lorraine No, it's all right, thank you…
Liz Don't be so daft, I'll give you a lift.

Lorraine stops and turns and they look at each other

Lorraine and Liz exit

We see Helen and Don. He sits, she is lying on her back, reading a book, her bare feet up on his lap. He absently massages her foot as he also reads a book. Silence for a moment

Helen (*still reading*) What?
Don (*still reading*) What?
Helen (*still reading*) You said something.
Don (*still reading*) I said… (*He turns back a page in the book to read*) "When you come to the end of a contraction, give a deep sigh and a great big smile".
Helen (*still reading*) Fat bloody chance of that. (*She sighs heavily and looks round the book at her stomach*) Look at me. I'm the size of a wardrobe. I should be claiming a disability pension. (*She goes back to her reading*) I suppose Wendy looked like she'd just swallowed a pickled walnut.
Don (*ignoring this, quoting from the book*) Here's a good one: "There is no special advice for this month of pregnancy other than to look after oneself in a sensible sort of way".
Helen Like what?
Don (*reading*) "Like no mountain climbing or other perilous sports".

Pause

Helen (*of her book*) It says here that men are more likely to think about sex when they're riding a bicycle than women are.

Pause

Don Women are what?
Helen Riding a bike, I suppose.

Pause. She sets her book aside

Helen You know what *is* supposed to be good for my condition? According to madam. Squatting, curry and orgasms.

He looks at her and then deliberately sets aside his book

Don Right. You have a squat, I'll nip out for a takeaway and we'll see what develops. (*He goes back to his book and his massaging*)

She goes back to her book

> *We see Caro sitting, writing her diary. She doesn't see Chris enter. He wears an unbuttoned raincoat and is slightly drunk*

He stands looking at her, then quietly moves to stand behind her, and bends

Chris (*into her ear but not loudly*) What-ho, fatty.

She jumps and will protectively close her diary as he leans his chin on her shoulder and will leave it there

Caro Honestly, Chris, and please don't call me fatty.

He has joined in on the "don't call me fatty" ... so that we should gather it to be a lighthearted routine, but in fact she is privately upset at what are constant references to her size. He kisses the side of her neck briefly and stands upright

Chris And how are we today—Mrs Chubs and her unlicked cub—still kicking the shit out of you, is he?
Caro Actually, he has been a bit rowdy—mind you, he always is after I've been to my exercise class.
Chris Oh, you've been to another *class*—wonderful! Oh yes, my mother sends her love—was it her love? Yes, it was her love—we had lunch—yes, I forgot to tell you she was coming up for the day—sorry—anyway, nothing exciting to report—just the usual "are you wearing a clean vest and when did you last apologise to your Maker"— (*he picks up the diary*) what's this?
Caro (*taking it from him*) Oh—just a book.
Chris What sort of book?
Caro Just a sort of—journal, that's all.
Chris Oh, a "journal", is it—let's have a look, then.
Caro (*lightly*) Certainly not.
Chris Oh, we've got secrets, have we?
Caro Just—thoughts, that's all, and why do you keep saying "Oh" all the time—have you been drinking? (*Again she makes it light but inwardly she is finding herself a little afraid of the way their relationship has developed this edge*)

Act II   55

Chris Thoughts about what?
Caro (*more awkwardly than she would like*) I'm just—writing down—every day—what I feel—about—having my first baby. Because ... it will never be the same, will it, not even if we have six it will never quite be the same ... and I shall want to remember.

A slight moment

Chris *Our* first baby. (*He smiles*)
Caro That's what I mean, you know it is.

His smile widens but is just as empty

Chris I've been thinking, by the way: I shan't be of any real use till he's about three, which according to Mama is just about par for the course. I'm sure you won't mind—I just want you to know I've been thinking about it. (*He holds the smile and then moves away from her*)

She remains sitting, not looking at him. So that they are together but apart

We see Paul alone, looking worried

Stuart enters breezily ... sees him

Stuart Hallo there ... you're one of the dads, incher? How's it going?
Paul Yeah, it's—er—yeah, it's good. Great.
Stuart First one, is it?
Paul Yeah—yeah, our first.
Stuart Bit scarey, eh? I mean, it's right what they say, innit? You need a licence to watch the telly or ride a motor bike or even do a bitta fishing, but a baby, you just take it home and drive it away.
Paul (*with his typical bravado*) Yeah—well—we're gonna be—you know—we're gonna be all right.

Which Stuart sees straight through

Stuart 'Course you are. You going to the Fathers Only class?
Paul When is it?
Stuart Thursday week.
Paul Yeah ... yeah, I might well do that.
Stuart Very informative it is, you'll enjoy it.
Paul Lorraine—that's my wife—she goes to all the other classes.
Stuart So does my Vicki. She loves her classes. In fact, I think that's the only

reason she keeps getting pregnant, to educate herself. You sure you're all right?
Paul Me? Yeah—great—why?
Stuart You look a bit—you know—a bit worried.
Paul No, I'm fine.
Stuart Tell you what—fancy a pint? I'm Stuart, by the way, how d'you do? (*He extends a hand*)

They shake hands

Paul Paul... (*Out of desperation, he decides to go for it*) The thing is ... why I'm looking a bit—you know—I forgot to go to the bank and the machine's playing up and I can't get any out and I'm supposed to be meeting this fellah later on to get some stuff for the new flat an' that, so I'm a bit stuck.
Stuart How much d'you need? (*He's already digging for his wad*)
Paul No, I couldn't.
Stuart How much?
Paul No—honest.
Stuart How—much?
Paul Well... I really need about forty or fifty.
Stuart Yeah, I can do that—I done some work for cash today.
Paul You're sure? I mean...
Stuart Sure I'm sure— (*lightly*) you're not gonna run away, are you?
Paul (*trying a smile back*) Course I'm not.
Stuart (*sorting out fifty pounds from his wad of used notes*) Waddaya think of the name Kieron?
Paul Very nice.
Stuart Kieron Cope. It's got a definitely classy ring to it, that has—there y'go, fifty notes—we'll have that pint then—right?
Paul I'm paying.
Stuart Too bloody right you're paying...

They move to exit

Stuart What are you calling yours?
Paul We haven't decided yet.
Stuart Don't let 'em give you any of that "a rose by any other" stuff—names are very important. For example, did you know that Nelson's real name was Horace? Horace—Nelson. And why d'you think Harold Wilson whose real name was Jim, called his son Giles?
Paul Harold who?

Paul and Stuart exit

Act II

The women and Patrick enter

We are in the exercise class

Jan I know you can't plan a labour but I'm preparing myself as much as I can to have a natural childbirth.
Vicki *Right.*
Patrick But we're also preparing ourselves for the fact that things could happen which necessitate involving the doctors and whatever they have to offer.
Vicki *Right.*
Jan It's really having a positive attitude and treating it all as a positive experience—don't you think?
Vicki Me? Oh—yeah—*right.*
Liz Never stops kicking me... (*she prods her bulge*) ...do you?
Lorraine What, all day you mean, or just at certain times?
Liz Whenever it fancies. Kick kick kick. It's almost impossible to hold a decent conversation—I mean if someone's kicking you, you're apt to lose concentration, right?
Lorraine Have you tried singing? That's what settles mine down: I sing to them.
Liz Oh yeah, I can see me doing that.
Lorraine It does work though. (*To Vicki*) Doesn't it?
Vicki Well, it did with my Jeremy. Trouble was, he got hooked on it and three o'clock every morning he's waking me up and I'm having to bash out half an hour of *I Did It My Way.*
Helen It's the size of me: I can't believe it. My husband has to haul me out of bed every morning. He calls himself The Winch.
Caro I like all that... I find it fascinating the way the body changes ... the way it—accommodates.
Liz (*with a slightly sarcastic edge*) What about your fella—does he find it fascinating?
Caro (*a little too brightly*) Chris? Chris is terrific. (*She changes the subject*) Excuse me, everyone... Ruth's going to be a bit late and asked if I'd start the class, so if that's all right with everyone, I suggest we go straight into our pelvic floor exercise...

They will all get into the squatting position ... looking straight ahead ... pulling in and out with the same sort of look on their faces as the cat has when it is emptying its bowels and trying to pretend it isn't ... as Caro continues

Feet apart, easy squatting on our toes, leaning forward on to our hands, keeping arms and back straight and knees wide apart ... and we draw up and tighten our pelvic floor muscles and we hold for as long as we can and we relax and we continue, breathing in as we tighten and breathing slowly out as we let go and we ... relax ... that's very good, Patrick, very good indeed, look at Patrick, everybody.

The others stonily regard Patrick

And going on we pull in and we hold ... and we relax ... we take it up ... and we let it down ... imagining we're a lift in Selfridges ... and we take it up to menswear on the first floor and we hold it and we take it down to household goods and kitchenware and we have a quick look around and we take it up again ... and we see how long we can hold it...
Helen In menswear.
Caro In menswear, yes—and we hold it as long as we can ... and we stop and how many of us managed to hold it for a count of five?

All the hands go up

Ten?

Jan's and Patrick's hands go up

More than ten?

Patrick's hand goes up

Jolly good and once again, please...
Lorraine Excuse me... I need to go to the toilet—sorry.
Others (*chorus, pointing*) Down the corridor, first on the right!
Lorraine Sorry.

Lorrain exits

Caro And now if we could go on to our rocking exercise, which if you remember is especially helpful in the prevention of backache...

They assume the "rocking" posture, leaning forward on their elbows, buttocks in the air ... and will rock to a chorus of "rock ... rock ... rock" ... but:

Oh yes ... and she did ask if there's anyone other than Chris and I who've made the decision to breastfeed?

Patrick's hand goes up instantly ... then Jan's

Act II

Caro What about you, Vicki?
Vicki Not this time, no—we've decided to bring in a caterer.

They continue with their exercises

Patrick exits

We see Paul, in work overalls, standing holding a letter as he uses a pay phone

Paul It's about your letter, Mr Hatton. About the flat. The thing is, Mr Hatton, I was wondering if you could give us another month. Yes, I know I signed an agreement, but I didn't think and it's a bit difficult what with the babies and everything—I mean there's no problem, I've already got my eye on another place, somewhere bigger in a very nice area, I mean, we'll have to have somewhere bigger in any case, it's just that, well, I've been let down you see and I need a bit more time... (*He listens and almost closes his eyes in relief*) Two months. Thank you, Mr Hatton, I really appreciate it, Mr Hatton, thank you. Oh, and Mr Hatton, sorry to ask you, but I mean I don't want her upset or anything, you know, not just now, so when the man comes for the rent if you could make sure he ... thank you, thank you very much, Mr Hatton. (*He replaces the receiver and almost closes his eyes in relief*)
Caro And relax.

Paul and all the women other than Lorraine will exit

Lorraine stands, looking around appreciatively

Liz enters with two mugs of tea, gives one to Lorraine

Lorraine (*of her surroundings*) It's really nice. Really nice.
Liz Yes, it's not a bad little place, I'm growing quite fond of it.
Lorraine It's lovely.

Pause. Liz breaks it

Liz This'll make you laugh: I spent the whole weekend scrubbing it from top to bottom, cupboards, carpets, the lot. I think they call it the nesting instinct. Me.

They smile at each other

Look, I hope you won't be offended but... (*She takes up some packages*)

people keep sending me things for the baby and I've already got far too much and...
Lorraine No. Thanks ever so much ... but no, I couldn't.
Liz But why, if I...
Lorraine ...because we've got all we need and what we haven't got we'll wait for. (*And she lightens it*) Anyway, you don't know my Paul.
Liz Has to be the provider, is that it?
Lorraine (*smiling*) 'Spose so, yes.
Liz Oh, come on, Lorraine, those days are...
Lorraine ...like you want to scrub floors, he wants to provide—that's all.

This moment between them

Liz Lorraine—it doesn't ... it doesn't pay to depend on someone so ... so completely.
Lorraine You mean Paul.
Liz What I mean is ... no-one can be completely dependable—no matter how much they...
Lorraine ...you mean I shouldn't trust him.
Liz No, I don't mean that—I mean... I just worry that you... I just wish you were that little bit more your own woman.
Lorraine Like you, you mean.
Liz No, not like me, like...
Lorraine I love him, Elisabeth. And he loves me. I *know* I can depend on him.

Pause

Song 11: Live Your Own Life

Liz
Here you are
Hiding regrets
Living on promises
Piling up debts
Performing your duty
Content with your life
There's more to a woman
Than being a wife

Lorraine
I'm happy with him
I'm happy with me
What I am
Is what you see
We'll see it through
We'll both survive

Act II

Liz　　　　You have your own future
　　　　　　You have your own life
　　　　　　First you're a woman
Lorraine　No! first I'm a wife
Liz & Lorraine Things don't change
　　　　　　Things go on
Lorraine　Most of them right
Liz　　　　But some of them wrong
Liz & Lorraine We're different people
　　　　　　It's plain to see
Lorraine　A wife
Liz　　　　A *woman*!
Liz & Lorraine For you not for me

Lorraine	It's easy to say	**Liz**	Here you are
	Not easy to do		Tying your hands
	Not for me		Denying ambition
	Maybe for you		Your own private plans
	I'd find it hard		No-one said it was easy
			Or free from strife
			Be your own woman

Liz & Lorraine Live your own life

　　　　　　No rags to riches
　　　　　　No magic wands
　　　　　　No rainbow's end
　　　　　　No golden ponds
　　　　　　No easy answers
　　　　　　Don't we agree
　　　　　　Both of us women
Liz　　　　But one who can't see

Lorraine	I'm happy with him	**Liz**	Here you are
	I'm happy with me		Nowhere to go
	What I am		A slave to convention
	Is what you see		With nothing to show
	We'll see it through		Think of your future
	We'll both survive		As more than a wife

Liz & Lorraine Be your own woman
　　　　　　Live your own life

The other women enter

We are in the exercise class. Each woman is doing a different exercise. Vicki is sitting on a chair, reading a small pamphlet as she vaguely raises one leg and then the other. Liz will join the others, but Lorraine will stay where she is, looking ahead, during the following

Jan A friend of mine had the most amazing birth, listening to Mozart and squatting in her partner's arms.

The dialogue is punctuated by their physical efforts

Caro Although they do say an epidural's super, you don't feel *anything*, it sort of paralyses you from the waist down.
Liz I don't want to be paralysed from the waist down, thank you.
Jan Absolutely. I want to be aware, not drugged out of my mind.
Caro Yes, I do know that some women feel cheated if there's no pain.
Helen Not me: I can't even stand having my legs waxed. What I want is a real high-tech with everything that's available: just wake me when the hairdresser arrives.
Jan Oh no, sorry, unless there's any sort of problem I want the message direct, not through instruments.
Liz Yes, I'm not sure I want it full of drugs before it's even born.
Caro Not that I think it will come to that in my case: I've always been a very physical type of person.
Vicki (*reading*) "When going into hospital or wherever... remember to take your Sony Walkman, your Scrabble set and so on".
Helen How can I scream and play Scrabble at the same time?
Liz I always scream when I play Scrabble.
Caro The thing to remember, surely, is that it's not like cancer or something ... in this case the pain has something at the end of it.
Helen I'll just jot that down on the back of my eyeballs so I don't forget...
Jan No, she's right, it's *positive* pain.
Caro The one to ask surely is Vicki.

They all stop and look towards Vicki who is vaguely exercising her legs. She stops

Vicki Don't look at me, I don't know what you're all on about: I thought natural childbirth was when you didn't wear make-up. (*But*) Just try and do what's right for *you*, that's all I can tell you.

A moment and they go back to their exercising

Liz It's not the pain I'm afraid of. It's making a fool of myself.

Act II

A moment as they dwell in this thought

Don enters, to a roll of drums. He wears a smart suit

The women exit as the men enter, US

Don moves DC *and, with the drum rolls and in the mode of a stage magician, slowly takes out his pocket handkerchief... to reveal it as a white nappy. He holds it up to the audience... this side, that side... then moves to where the other men are loosely grouped around a table... takes up a baby doll and, with deft competence and the accompanying drumroll, puts the nappy on it and triumphantly holds it up for inspection. The other men applaud. Don lowers the doll and, in doing so, bangs its head against the table, thus breaking the mood. Chris has remained very much on the edge of things, making it clear that he finds the whole thing a waste of time*

Don And the next gentleman, please.

Patrick quickly steps in. He will change the nappy, watched and coached by some of the others, as Paul manages a discreet word with Stuart

Paul I've been really stupid, I've forgot my wallet.
Stuart Don't worry about it.
Paul Yeah, but I don't want you to think...
Stuart ...don't *worry*—OK? (*He smiles*)

Paul manages a smile back

Chris (*to Don*) You do know what all this is about, don't you?
Don All what?
Chris The way they try to involve us ... the way they try to make us feel necessary ... the way we kid ourselves by reading books and learning to change nappies and generally being "a jolly good chap" ... because *they* know and deep down inside *we* know that once we've done the deed, once we've set the jolly old seed rolling, we're biologically redundant. They don't need us any more.
Don (*flatly*) Is that right?
Chris (*grinning*) That isn't to say that we don't play the game. Or try to. Most of us, anyway. Mustn't let the side down, old chap, mustn't moan, mustn't be anything less than totally supportive...

He is aware that the others are now listening to him

I mean, is there any one of us here who, if he's really honest, can say he's never felt the need to be—disloyal ... to be something other than an Optional Extra?

Don Sure. Who hasn't? I just try to hang on to the thought that it's my baby too ... she just happens to be lumbered with carrying it. (*He "smiles"*)

Chris returns the smile, quite aware that he is not exactly Mr Popular and not displeased by the knowledge

Chris (*smiling broadly*) Anyway—I'm off—good night all.
Stuart (*flatly*) You'll miss the film show.
Chris Yes and I'm sure it will be absolutely fascinating, but unfortunately I've got to dash off and watch some paint dry. (*He makes to go*) Oh—good luck on The Day.

Chris exits

Pause

Paul What was all that about? (*He hasn't really understood the exchange but has found it disturbing*)
Stuart Sounds to me like someone who's a bit umpty at the prospect of sharing his trainset— (*he is aware that Paul is disturbed and so gets his attention*) Right then, Houdini, let's sort this lot out.

Paul and Patrick will concentrate on the nappy as

Don (*admitting, despite himself*) It's true to some extent: you *can* feel left out of it at times—I mean how *do* you share something that's mostly going on inside them—and truth is they don't always want you to. You've just got to take it a day at a time. Hope you don't make the wrong noises.
Paul I know it's gonna be painful and I get really scared for her. I'm gonna be there, course I am, I mean I wouldn't not be there... I just hope... I just hope I can cope. See ... part of me thinks it's wonderful and part of me is dead-scared. (*He moves away from the others*) Sometimes I ... sometimes I don't know which way to turn. (*He stands, looking out, as though into the future*)

Don and Stuart exchange glances

Don It'll be all right. I promise you.
Paul (*bucking himself up*) Oh—yeah—sure—course it will—I'm looking forward to it—you know, being a dad an'that.
Patrick (*holding up the doll and looking it straight in the glass eye*) I want to get to know my child as soon as possible.

Paul (*seriously*) Right.
Patrick And for my child to get to know *me*.
Don The only time I ever got anywhere near understanding *my* old man was when I had a kid of my own.
Stuart *Right*. And I still thought he was a wanker.
Patrick The thing being, of course, that so often we repeat the ways our own parents brought us up—which in my case, I'm afraid, left rather a lot to be desired.
Paul Yeah, but I mean ... you can learn from it, can't you? Things about your own parents that you ... you know. You can say ... "I'll never do that, I'll do it right".
Patrick The thing to do surely is to compare childhoods with your partner to iron out any ... areas of disagreement.

Stuart is aware that all this chat is increasing Paul's uneasiness and so changes the subject

Stuart Abso-bloody-lutely, Patrick, my old jar of chutney—now come on, have another go at Ada here so you can impress Harpoon Annie when she gets back.

Patrick will have another go at the nappy, watched and coached by Stuart as Don moves to Paul

Paul I mean ... you're bound to make *some* mistakes—I mean nobody's—nobody's perfect, are they? And I mean ... even if a father *does* make mistakes it don't mean he doesn't love his kids, does it? It don't mean he doesn't love them.

A slight pause

Don No. That much I can promise you.

There is a short burst of noise from the others as Patrick gets it all wrong

Stuart Give us a hand, will you, Donald?

Don smiles at Paul, giving a little jerk of the head towards the others and moves over to assist in instructing Patrick. Paul moves away from them, so that he is alone

Music

Song 12: My Dad

Paul I didn't know my dad
Not the way I should
I know he tried his best, my dad
Did everything he could

'Course, things were different then
For people like my dad
He didn't have a lot of things
That other people had

I'd like to see my dad
I'm told we look the same
Mum says he is bad, my dad
Won't even speak his name

Now I'm to be a dad
I bet he'd like to know
He'll be a grandad soon, my dad
Why'd he have to go?

He didn't want to leave, my dad
I bet he even cried
He said "I'll always love you, lad"
He never would've lied
My dad

The music ends

The men will exit as we see Caro in a chair, under a duvet. She is awake

Chris enters furtively

He looks into a mirror, wiping his mouth with a handkerchief, checking for lipstick. He is wearing the same coat as in the previous scene. He pockets the handkerchief and moves towards Caro. Hearing him, she turns on her side and pretends to be sleeping. He stands looking down at her. After a moment she turns, as though disturbed, and looks at him

Chris Sorry.
Caro (*knowing full-well*) What time is it?
Chris Half eleven.
Caro (*reaching a hand up to him*) What was it like?

Act II

Chris (*taking her hand*) Yeah, it was—OK.

She pulls on his hand for him to kiss her ... which he does, on the mouth, but quickly, and then lets her hand go

(*Taking off his coat*) Went on a bit—the what's-her-name, the midwife gave us a pep talk, then there was some practical stuff and then she ran the film—the one you saw I imagine—then some of us went over to that wine bar for a drink—that's why I'm a bit late.
Caro Have you eaten?
Chris Some sort of chicken thing. (*He makes to go out, taking off his jacket, as though to the bathroom*)
Caro Chris...
Chris (*quickly, guiltily*) Yes?
Caro I'm glad you went.

Pause

Chris Yes. Well... (*He sits, his back to her*)

Caro lies with her eyes open

We see Liz, lying on a duvet, DL, *trying to get comfortable. She looks at the audience*

Liz I can't bend, I can't paint my toenails, I can't shave my legs, I can't do anything. You don't know what a relief it is to sit in the bath with water over my stomach. Right. (*She lies down and tries to get comfortable*)

We see Jan sitting in a chair, in a nightgown, under a duvet

Patrick enters with a tray

Jan (*surprised*) What's this?
Patrick Good wholesome food.
Jan I mean what are you doing home?
Patrick I've taken the week off.
Jan What for?
Patrick To look after you.
Jan How many *more* weeks are you going to take off?
Patrick As many as it needs to look after you.
Jan I don't *need* looking after.
Patrick The doctor said...

Jan ...the doctor said I should put my feet up for a couple of days... he didn't say my husband should give up work to look after me... I've already given up work ... one of us should be working, Patrick, or this child if it ever deigns to put in an appearance will be living off blackberries.

Patrick OK, that's fine, you've got rid of your hostility which is based on your interpretation of my behaviour as a threat to our child—all of which we'll discuss later, OK—now eat some of this soup.

Jan I don't want your soup! Your soup is disgusting, it always *was* disgusting! I am not sick, I am pregnant and I don't need soup, what I need is space, I'm tired of you hanging over me all the time, I'm tired of being treated like the sacred cow—I may look like a cow but I still feel like *me*—go away, I don't want you here, go away! (*She raises the soup spoon as though to throw at him*)

Patrick exits hurriedly

Jan sits glowering

We see Helen. She lies on the floor at the foot of the bed, face down with her head on her folded arms and her knees bent so that her behind sticks up in the air

Don enters, jacketless and loosening his tie

During the following, he will lie on the bed, looking disgruntled

Helen I said to her ... listen, Madam Physio or whatever your name is ... before all this, my idea of exercise was to get up in the middle of the night and illegally use my hosepipe.

Don Do you *have* to sit like that?

Helen Why, what's wrong with it?

Don Well, it's not very ladylike, is it?

Helen It may not be very ladylike but it's incredibly comfortable. I know what you mean though: I used to have this recurring dream where I'd stopped work and from then on spent all day long lying in a hammock under a tree reading books with a halo over my head—instead of which, look at me. I told you—I'm a freak—an ugly freak—half-woman, half-frog—you do know that I'm having the world's first twenty-four month pregnancy?

Don Yeah, all right Helen, all right.

Sharp enough for her to sense trouble

Helen (*without looking at him*) What's wrong?

Act II

Don Nothing's wrong. (*But*) I tell you what's wrong—I've had a long day, I've got a lot on my mind. What I needed was to relax, not to sit here staring at your behind while you go on and on about what a freak you are, about how ugly you are. I keep telling you, you're not a freak and you're not ugly, you're pregnant.
Helen Oh—yes—well of course—you'd know all about that.
Don I know enough to know what it's *like* so I don't need...
Helen ...you know what it was like with *her*...
Don ...that's what I'm trying to tell you, it's the *same*...
Helen It is *not* the same, I am not her, I am me!

Pause

Is this the time to start a row?
Don Is this the time to start a family? For chrissake, I'm fifty years old, I thought I was finished with all that. Has it ever occurred to you that by the time he's twenty I shall be seventy? I mean, that's really something to look forward to—for all of us.

It's the first time he's ever said anything like this and it comes as a complete stunner

Helen If you didn't want this baby, you should have said so.
Don I wanted it because I love you and because *you* wanted it—and if you want the truth... if you really want the truth, I didn't think you'd go through with it but I wanted the decision to come from you, not me. (*Immediately, he regrets what he has said*)

She has remained in the crouching position throughout. Now, after a moment, she moves awkwardly so that she is sitting on the floor, but still away from him

I didn't mean that. I really didn't mean that.

Pause

Paul and Lorraine enter during the following

Song 13: Look at Me
Don Look at me
I've never felt like this before
She is all I need
And have never wanted more

	Before this happened
	Things were fine
	I was hers
	She was mine
	But this could make a difference
	Can it ever be the same?
Paul	Will it be all right
Chris	Will she still love me
Paul & Chris	Will there be time
	For her to love me?
Don	Or will I find that
	Nothing's quite the same
Paul	I'm insecure
Chris	And I'm not sure
	I like this man you see
Don & Chris & Paul	I am lost
	Look at me
Lorraine	Look at me
	I've got what I'd been praying for
	And I know he
	Has feelings that are just as sure
Caro	We've enjoyed success
	In all we've done
	Our lives fulfilled
	We've had our fun
Helen	Now it all seems so different
	Can it be that way again
Caro	Will it work out right?
	Will he still love me?
	No, what I mean is
	Will he need me?
Helen	Could I have seen that
	Things might have to change
	I know that I
	Can't justify
	The way I seem to be
Helen & Caro	I feel lost
	Look at me
Paul	Perhaps we should have waited
	For another year

Act II

Lorraine   This is what we wanted
   And it's almost here
Chris & Don   I wonder why it's affecting me this way
Caro   He can't deny he's rejecting me
Men   Can't find the key
Caro & Helen   Why can't he see
Men   Look at me

Don & Helen   Look at us
   We've never been like this before
Chris & Caro   We no longer discuss
   The moment we've been striving for

Lorraine & Paul   It's funny how
   We try so hard
Helen & Don   But somehow seem
   To disregard
   That it could make a difference
All   Someone else in our lives
Caro & Chris   Will it be all right
   Will they both love me?
Caro & Chris & Lorraine & Paul   It's up to me
   To make them love me
Helen & Don   We must accept
   That things will have to change
All   If we can't share
   And in despair
   We fight and disagree
   Then we're lost
   Look at us
   Look at me

The music ends

We see Vicki and Caro together at the hospital

Vicki Listen—we all get the jitters round about this time—you want to hear me and my old man. No, it's this little darling… (*She indicates her bulge*) It's bound to put a strain on things, innit?
Caro I thought… silly of me, really… I thought it was different for someone like you.
Vicki What, you so uptight and me just breezing through it, oh dear, oh lor', I'm pregnant again—right?

Caro (*smiling*) Right.
Vicki Yeah, well, can't say as I blame you. Fancy another coffee?
Caro Let me get it.
Vicki (*levering herself up*) No, no, you waddled over last time.
Caro D'you think I might have an orange juice?
Vicki Orange juice. Right. (*She makes to go*) Don't think because my babies come easy they don't mean much. Whoever I'm carrying in here will be as loved and as precious and as welcome as the two that came before her were and as any that come after her will be. (*She "paws the ground" and cups a hand to her mouth to shout*) Stand back, I'm coming through!

Vicki exits, with an exaggerated waddle

We see Liz and Lorraine

Lorraine D'you ever see him—you know...
Liz "The Father of My Child"? No, thank God.
Lorraine I don't know how you can say that...
Liz ...It's very simple. I don't want anything to do with him...
Lorraine ...But it's his baby...
Liz ...No, it's my baby, he's more than happy to leave it that way, and if I'm stuck with bringing up a kid, I'm more than happy to be doing it in an environment which is totally free from masculine values. (*She permits herself a smile*) So there.
Lorraine See, for me, that's what it's all about ... being with someone you love ... sharing with someone you love...
Liz ...Yes, well, bully for you: I happen to be one of these women who doesn't feel incomplete without a man—sorry but there *are* some of us around. More and more as it happens. (*She finds herself angry and moves away*) All right. I don't... I don't seem to have a talent for "long term and fulfilling relationships", or anyway that's how it seems. To have anything worthwhile, you need commitment... *I* need commitment and that's something else I seem to...
Lorraine How can you have a baby by someone you don't want to be with...?
Liz The baby was a mistake...
Lorraine ...But how could you do it...
Liz I've told you, the baby was a...
Lorraine ...then you should have stopped it...
Liz ...Lorraine...
Lorraine ...shouldn't you, you should have stopped it...
Liz ...you don't understand...
Lorraine ...no, I don't because I'm not very clever and I'm glad really,

Act II

Elisabeth, because it probably takes a very clever woman to talk the way you do about the baby that's inside of her ... excuse me, I have to go home now.
Liz I'll take you.
Lorraine No, I just want to go home. (*She makes to exit*)
Liz I had a baby before. Five years ago. The—father was married. He said he was going to leave her. I was six months gone before he—changed his mind. He—refused to have any more to do with me. They told me it was too late to bring about a termination and so I—took matters into my own hands. Without success. The baby was born prematurely and lived for three days. I don't intend to kill this child, no matter how I feel about its father. And... I want it, you see... I want it.

We see Vicki who sits, lost in rather uneasy thoughts ... which she hides as Stuart enters with some children's toys

Vicki They all right?
Stuart Fast asleep.

During the following, he will put the toys in a box

Vicki Jasmine.
Stuart No.
Vicki Why not?
Stuart Because I hate the name Jasmine and what is more I knew a bloke called Jasmine and I hated *him* an'all. (*He bends over to kiss the top of her head*) Fancy something to eat? I could do you one of my omelettes.
Vicki (*reaching her hand up to him*) In a minute, p'r'aps.

He sits on the floor next to her. She reaches down to gently touch his face. He takes her hand and kisses it gently, and remains holding her hand

(*After a pause*) It feels different.
Stuart How d'you mean—different?

During the following, he turns and gently puts his hand on her belly

Vicki Just ... different. From the other two.
Stuart Well, he's not in a hurry to come out, I know that much... (*He leans his head against her belly*) Hallo, old mate, how's it going in there? Having a good time, are you? (*He pretends to listen*) He says he's a bit fed up with hanging around and can you swallow some Lego so he's got something to play with?

But Vicki is still lost in her own uneasy thoughts. He realizes. A slight moment

You're not worried, are you?
Vicki That'll be the day.

Stuart and Vicki exit

We see Chris, smartly-dressed, his back to us, furtively using the phone

Caro (*off*) Chris?
Chris I've got to go ... look—I'll be there in half an hour—bye.

He replaces the receiver as Caro enters with a bag

She smiles at him. We should sense a tension between them. She puts down the bag and takes out a pile of new baby clothes. She holds up a tiny growsuit ... holds it to her, unable to resist thinking of the baby that will soon be wearing it. She becomes aware that Chris is looking at her and gives him a tentative smile

Caro (*of the growsuit*) What d'you think?

Pause

Chris What do I think? (*He tosses the paper aside*) I think it's perfect. Like you. Perfect. Everything's perfect. I'm surrounded by perfection. What an incredibly lucky fellow I am. (*He gives her his flat smile*)

She tries to smile back ... but turns away, busying herself unnecessarily with the clothing. Pause

(*Getting up briskly*) I have to go to a meeting. I did tell you.
Caro Yes. Yes, you did. (*She again tries the smile and continues to busy herself*)
Chris I don't know what time I'll be back, it's bound to go on.

She nods, smiles, but is unable to look at him. This moment. We should sense that he knows he is being a shit but is somehow unable to control it

You'll be all right, will you?
Caro Oh God, yes, heaps to do.
Chris Yes ... well... (*He almost makes a smart-arsed remark but instead is about to go*)

Act II

Caro Chris...

He turns. Music

Chris Yes?

They look at each other ... each wanting the other to say something to bring what is happening to them out into the open ... but she shakes her head and turns away, busies herself

Well?
Caro (*shaking her head, not looking at him*) It doesn't matter.

Song 14: Ask Me

Chris	Ask me where I'm going
	Ask me
	Ask me
	Ask me who I'm seeing
Caro	I don't want to know
Chris	Ask me who I'm meeting
	Ask me
	Ask me
	Ask me if I'm cheating
Caro	If you're going, please go
Chris	Tell me you despise me
	Say it, say *something*
	Tell me that you...
Caro	...Please, I've asked you to go
Chris	Why won't you ever face it?
	Come on—face it
	Why is it you can't...
Caro	I've told you
	I've told you
	I don't want to hear it
Caro/Chris	I don't want to hear it
	I don't want to know
Chris	You really are special
	So calm, so discreet
	So wise, so maternal,

	So bloody complete
	A shining example
	Of all we should be
Caro	Please stop this, Chris, stop it
	Don't do this to me

	You know that I love you	**Chris**	Let's face it, perfection Is your middle name
	I'm proud of your name		You and my mother Exactly the same
	You find another Who'd love you the same		You're always assessing So bloody depressing And no points for guessing Who's always to blame

Caro Blame for *what*?
Tell me—*what*?

Chris	I'm behaving so badly?
	Oh, dear what a shame
Caro	We're having a baby
	Not playing a game
Chris	Oh... So glad I'm included
	So glad you said *we*

Caro All right!
The child that's in you
Fears the child that's in me

The music stops, unresolved as they look at each other, each shocked by the truth of what she has said, and then—as though afraid

Caro	Tell me that you love me
	Tell me tell me
	Tell me that you love me
Chris	You don't want to know
	Ask me where I'm going
	Ask me ask me
	Ask me who I'm seeing
Caro	I don't want to know

	Tell me that you love me	**Chris**	Ask me who I'm meeting
	Tell me tell me		Ask me ask me

Act II

> Tell me that you love me
> I don't want to know

> Ask me if I'm cheating
> You don't want to know

Chris and Caro look at each other

We see Jan, very heavy now, doing her "pushing" exercises

Patrick enters

Jan (*between her breathing*) Where did you disappear to?
Patrick I thought I'd check the hospital run. (*He sits*)
Jan (*heaving herself up off the floor*) You did that yesterday.
Patrick Yes, I know, but that was in the rush hour.
Jan How long?
Patrick Eighteen minutes door to door.
Jan Eighteen minutes.
Patrick Door to door.
Jan That's good, isn't it?
Patrick I'll do it again later, just to double-check.
Jan Patrick...

And she sits on his lap so that he almost disappears under her

> I just want you to know ... that I love you very much. I just want you to know ... that I'm very happy. In fact ... this is the happiest time of my life... I just want you to know that. (*Suddenly she bursts into tears*) I'm so happy! (*She hugs him tighter*)

All we can see of him is his flailing legs and arms

> *We see Helen and Don lying in bed. She is trying to get comfortable, positioning pillows. He lies on his side, one arm thrown loosely across her, apparently oblivious to her restlessness*

Helen And if the breathing doesn't work, she says to try some form of distraction.
Don (*almost asleep*) Mmmm.
Helen (*re-positioning herself again*) Like ... a song ... like Ten Green Bottles ... or ... One Man Went to Mow ... something repetitive ... or the alphabet.
Don Mmmm.
Helen It's no good, I can't sleep, I'm going to make a cup of tea or something.

Don (*drowsily*) I'll do it.

She looks at him. He makes no attempt to move. She gets up and moves DC *and "moves a curtain" as though she is looking out of a window*

Pause

Music

Helen It's raining. We need a good storm ... clear the air. (*A moment as she remains looking out ... then she "writes" on the glass with her finger*) H.R. loves D.M. (*After a pause*) Most of the time. (*After a pause*) It wasn't a "romantic accident". This baby of ours. It was because of *her*. (*She smiles to herself*) Even the baby I'm carrying is because of *her*. (*After a slight pause*) Right up to the last minute we went on that holiday there was a drama—every week there was a drama—I can't remember a time when she wasn't phoning you or you weren't phoning her and I just sat tight and I thought, he'll let go, sooner or later he'll have to let go ... you even phoned her from the hotel, just to see if everything was "all right". And then that young family arrived and I watched you playing with their children and I saw the pain you felt at losing your own children and I thought that's the answer, that's what I'm going to do, I'm going to have a baby... I'm going to have a baby and it will be his and mine and nothing—*nothing*—to do with bloody Wendy.

Song 15: Nothing to Do with Wendy

This one little thing
One tiny thing
That's nothing to do with Wendy
There's just him and there's me
So why can't he see
It's nothing to do with her

That one fateful day
That one brief decision
And all I hear is Wendy
This child that I bear
This private affair
Has nothing to do with her

This child is his and mine
Not hers, no, it is his and mine
But he just can't say no

Act II

>Can't let her go
>I need to know

During the following, Don sits up

>That this one little thing
>This one tiny thing
>Means more to him than Wendy
>This child here in me
>Our life that's to be
>Is nothing to do with her

Pause as Don is looking at her. She uses the side of her hand to erase her window-writing, but, unseen by her, he moves to her

Don You forgot to put D.M. loves H.R.

She turns to see him

>All of the time. (*He embraces her*)

We see Paul reading a letter, worried

But he quickly stuffs it into his overalls pocket as Lorraine enters, wearily, carrying a shopping bag

He will immediately go and relieve her of the bag as:

Lorraine (*her face lighting up*) Oh, hallo, you're home early— (*suddenly concerned*) there's nothing wrong, is there, Paul?
Paul Why should there be something wrong?
Lorraine You don't usually come home dinner-time.
Paul (*masterfully*) Oi. (*Now it's his turn to be concerned*) Come on, sit down, you look really tired.

She sits, not unwillingly, as he tells one of his lies

>No, what it is, I'm taking out this insurance policy and I arranged to see the bloke this dinner-time.

Lorraine What insurance policy?
Paul I told you, I'm taking out a couple of insurance policies— (*he leans close to her; "heavily"*) so you'll be looked after. (*He is already on his way out, taking the bag*)

Lorraine Where you going now?
Paul Put the kettle on.

Paul exits

Lorraine (*calling*) There's some sausage rolls in the bag.
Paul (*off, calling*) Lovely—any pickle?
Lorraine Umm ... not sure. (*She sits and finds her eyes closing. After a moment, still with her eyes closed, and more to herself than to him*) One of the mothers brought in her new baby today—to show us how to put a nappy on and everything. It was just a few days old and oh, Paul, it was so small: small and crushed and bruised. I didn't realize just how small they are ... so small and so helpless and so ... trusting. (*She smiles at the memory. After a pause*) Paul... They want me to go into hospital.

A moment, and Paul appears

Paul Why?
Lorraine They say ... they say the babies are in the wrong place.
Patrick ...What do they mean, "wrong place"...?
Lorraine ...They're up here, under my ribs, that's why I've been getting those pains—but it's nothing to worry about, Paul, really—they just want to keep an eye on me and make sure I'm looking after myself. (*Even as she has said this last bit, she knows it is a mistake*)
Paul What d'you mean ... looking after yourself?

A slight pause

Lorraine They say the babies aren't as big as they should be—they don't think I'm eating enough, which is silly, but ... they say I shouldn't be so tired all the time...

Pause

And the lady from the office said she wants to speak to you.
Paul What lady.
Lorraine The lady from the hospital.
Paul What about?

She is clearly unwilling to say

Paul What *about*, Lolly?
Lorraine About where we're going to live.

Act II

Paul I've already *told* them I...
Lorraine ...You told them the landlord was putting us into a bigger flat. They telephoned him, Paul. He said he didn't know anything about no other flat. He said he wants us out of this flat because we haven't paid the rent for the past three months.
Paul I... I used the money as a deposit on another place.
Lorraine What other place, Paul?
Paul Look—he done a runner on me, OK?

Pause. He enmeshed in another one of his fantasies and she unwilling to challenge it

Lorraine She said they'd write another letter to the council.
Paul Why did they have to involve you? I *told* them—I didn't want you involved, I didn't want you worrying—and you don't have to worry, Lolly, because I'm not the sort who just lets things happen—OK? I've got ideas.
Lorraine But you see, Paul ... sometimes ideas aren't enough, sometimes you have to...
Paul (*a sudden outburst*) Listen!

They are both left not knowing what to say

(*In little more than a whisper*) Listen... (*He suddenly looks very young and very lost and totally unable to express what he wants to say. He turns his back on her, forcing back tears and not wanting her or anyone to see his despair*)

Lorraine will remain seated and Paul will remain with his back to her as Vicki enters, wearing paint-splattered overalls and headscarf, and carrying a large paintbrush

During the following, she climbs a pair of aluminium steps and is about to "paint" the ceiling

Music

Voice OK, ladies ... we've done our exercises ... we've practised our breathing ... we've read our books ... we've packed our little suitcases... Lights! Cameras! Action! The show is on!

The Lights change to the "un-naturalistic" state—and there will be a constant flow of activity—during which Paul will quietly exit—as Vicki carries on with her painting—and we see Patrick, sound asleep

Jan, in dressing gown, enters and wakens him gently

Song 16: It's Starting

Jan It's starting
Patrick (*drowsily*) What's happened?
Jan I think it's on its way
It's starting
Patrick What time is it? Four o'clock. (*He leaps up, scutting around, pulling trousers etc. on over his pyjamas*)
Jan We've finally hit the day
A life beginning
Patrick What can I do?
Jan My head is spinning
Patrick Tea! I'll make some tea.
Jan And as my pulse begins to race
My heart is leaping into space

She hands him his list, takes up a towel and makes to go

It's starting
Patrick (*worriedly*) Where are you going?
Jan I never felt so good
Patrick You're having a bath? There isn't time!
Jan Done everything I could

He falls over, trying to put a leg into his trousers

Jan (*laughing*) So spread the word to kith and kin
And get out that old violin
A life is about to begin.

Jan exits

Patrick continues to dress as Vicki stops painting, as her contractions—not the first—start. She sits on top of the steps, looking at her watch and counting under her breath

Vicki Nineteen minutes. (*She remains thus*)

We see Don and Helen. Both using phones. She is standing, he is sitting "at a desk"

During the following, Lorraine moves to sit on a bed

Act II

Helen They're different—regular—about every twenty minutes.
Don OK—don't panic—I'm on my way—you'd better phone the hospital and say we're coming. And you're OK.
Helen I'm fine.
Don You're sure?
Helen I'm positive—I love you.
Don And I love you.

They hang up

Don (*yelling*) Mrs Barber!
Woman (*off; calling*) Yes, Mr Masters?
Don This is it!

        It's starting
        The future can begin
Helen   It's starting
Don & Helen A life about to win
        A chance of glory
Helen   Another story
Don & Helen Another door into a world
        That's full of wonders yet unfurled

They make for the exit

        It's starting

Don and Helen exit—Don less calmly than Helen

Lorraine, on the bed, is gripped by a contraction and in turn is gripping at the bed

Lorraine It's starting… Oh! It's *hurting*!

Jan and Patrick enter with all their "birth paraphernalia" and will check it against their list during the following

Jan Ready? Tapes.
Patrick Check.
Jan Charts?
Patrick Check.
Jan Photographs?
Patrick Check.

Jan Joss sticks?
Patrick Check.
Jan Apple juice?
Patrick Check.
Jan Camomile and raspberry leaf tea?
Patrick Check.
Jan Rug?
Patrick Check.
Jan Bucket?
Patrick Bucket ... err, bucket.
Jan (*pointing to the bucket under her*) Check?
Patrick Check!

Jan, Vicki, Lorraine and Helen sing quietly as we see Liz using the phone

Jan & Vicki & Lorraine & Helen And now we're almost there
　　　　I'm in the clouds somewhere
　　　　I feel—unreal
　　　　Nothing can compare

Liz It's starting
　Spencer, Elisabeth Spencer.
　　　　It's starting.
About every ten to fifteen minutes. Yes, that's what I thought. No, there isn't. No, really—there's no need for that, I'll get a minicab. Yes. (*She "smiles"*) I look forward to seeing *you*, too. (*She hangs up and immediately re-dials for a cab*)

Vicki comes down the steps

Vicki (*calling*) Jeremy! Go and get your father—he's down the betting shop—tell him it's starting—then go and fetch your grandma and she'll make you a nice tea.

We see Caro, coming to the end of some contractions. She breathes heavily but tries to control it

Chris enters

A moment and Liz, Vicki, Lorraine, Jan & Patrick sing quietly at the same time as Chris and Caro

Liz & Vicki & Lorraine & Jan & Patrick It's starting

Act II

>   The future can begin
>   It's starting
>   A life about to win
>   A chance of glory
>   Another story
>   Another door into a world
>   That's full of wonders yet unfurled

Chris I—er—I'm just going to pop down to the pub for half an hour, OK?
Caro (*smiling*) Fine.
Chris I don't suppose you want to come.
Caro No. Thanks.

Pause

Chris Are you all right, you look…
Caro No, I'm fine. Just—uncomfortable.

Pause. He gives a little nod and is about to go

Chris Half an hour—all right?

She nods

Chris exits

Caro remains sitting, looking straight ahead

Liz & Vicki & Lorraine & Jan & Patrick It's starting
>   The time is getting near
Liz & Vicki & Lorraine & Jan & Patrick & Caro It's starting
Caro   There's nothing I should fear
All   So fingers crossed and on our way
>   For everything will be OK
>   For someone
>   Today is the day

Vicki collects steps and exits

Caro takes up a pen and pad to write

We see Don anxiously supporting Helen as she comes to the end of a contraction

Don That's every fifteen minutes. Time for us to go. (*He helps her to her feet*)

Helen You've got all the phone numbers and everything.
Don (*patting his pocket*) All done.
Helen (*after a pause*) Off we go then.
Don Off we go. (*He kisses her*)

Don and Helen exit

We see Caro finishing writing and preparing to leave, dressed in a topcoat, carrying a small suitcase. She places a folded note carefully on her chair

Patrick and Jan enter. She is wearing a raincoat over her nightdress, and carries a small suitcase. He carries a large rubber plant, a video recorder, the bucket and a canvas bag full of all their bits and pieces

Jan Everything in the car?
Patrick Check.
Jan Absolutely sure?
Patrick Check.
Jan Car keys? (*He's about to say "check" ... but his face changes and he tips out their baggage to search through everything for the keys*)

Helen and Don enter. She is carrying an overnight bag

During the following, Vicki enters with Stuart

Don takes the bag from Helen as Lorraine takes a deep breath

Lorraine (*managing a smile*) Soon be there.
Vicki & Helen Not long now.
Caro & Liz At last.
Jan This is it.
Men Let's go!

Helen, Don, Vicki, Stuart, Jan, Patrick, Caro, Liz and Lorraine all face front in their various positions and activities

All   It's starting
            I feel it's on its way
            It's starting
            We've finally hit the day
            A life beginning
            My head is spinning
            As my pulse begins to race
            My heart is leaping into space

Act II

>   It's starting
>   I never felt so good
>   It's starting
>   Did everything I could
>   Together we'll make such a team
>   Feel such relief I want to scream
>   Could this be the start of a dream
>
> **Women & Patrick** It's starting
>   The future can begin   **Men**   We've travelled quite
>   It's starting   a way
>   A life about to win   Since that eventful day
>   A chance of glory   You're great—first
>   Another story   rate
>   Another door in to a   Did I never say
>   world
>   That's full of wonders
>   yet unfurled
>
> **Women & Patrick** It's starting   **Men**   It's very nearly due
>   The time is here at last   Take care, I love you
>   It's starting
>   And things are moving
>   fast
> **All**   So spread the word to
>   kith and kin
>   And get out that old
>   violin
>   A life is about to begin
>
>   'Cos come what may, through thick and thin
>   A life is about to begin
>   It's starting!

They exit

Chris enters

Chris (*calling*) Caro? Caroline? (*He moves briskly across ... then stops, seeing a note, and taking it up to read*) Oh Christ... Christ!

The "hospital wall" comes in as Chris exits and Stuart enters, carrying a bunch of flowers

Stuart sees Paul hurrying to exit, carrying a suitcase. We have a "frontcloth" dialogue

Stuart Hallo there—where *you* off to?
Paul (*uneasily*) I was just ... you know.

Stuart instinctively knows that all is not well, but indicates the case Paul is carrying

Stuart What—it's started, has it?
Paul Yeah, I was just...
Stuart ...going to the hospital.
Paul Yeah, that's right ... going to the hospital.
Stuart Just as well I met you then, 'cos you're going the wrong way... (*He puts an arm round Paul*) Come on, son, it'll be all right. She's in safe hands, I promise you. I've been here before, remember. Now then, I'll give you a few tips ... one—don't make any jokes. She won't be in the mood for jokes. Two—prepare for some ripe old language. (*He gives the flowers to Paul*) Here y'are, present from me and Vicki. Come on, son, best foot forward.

*Paul and Stuart exit. Music 17 (***The Birth***) begins, underscoring the following dialogue*

Patrick enters

Patrick Excuse me, Doctor, but I want to make it known from the outset that I intend sharing this experience with my partner ... that is, I want to be with her for as much of the time as possible.
Jan (*off; yelling*) Patrick, where are you!

Patrick hurriedly exits behind the "wall"

Caro (*tunelessly*) One man went to mow went to mow...
Stuart (*as Doctor*) Now then ... anaesthetic...
Jan I'm not having an anaesthetic, thank you...
Stuart (*as Doctor*) Would you mind if some medical students watched the birth?
Liz Yes, I would bloody mind ... aahh!

Paul, Don and Stuart step outside the "wall" ... and pace, crossing each other

Don Do your breathing exercises... (*He demonstrates*)

Act II

Helen Who's having this baby, you or me?
Chris I want to share the pain with her and I can't...
Caro Hold my hand...
Chris She's all right, isn't she? I mean she's pulling the most terrible faces.
Caro I'm trying to smile, dammit! I'm trying to make you feel that I'm not feeling so bad! (*She gives a yell*)
Helen Z, Y, X, W, V, U, T, S...
Don Where's the anaesthetist! My wife needs an anaesthetic!
Jan No drugs! I don't want any drugs!
Vicki (*as Nurse*) Shouldn't we contact your husband, Mrs Ford?
Lorraine It's all right ... it's all right... (*But she cries out*) Paul!
Paul I'm here, Lolly, I'm here...
Helen This is all your fault—look at me! I shall never sleep with you again!
Patrick Keep singing ... keep singing...
    One man went to mow
    Went to mow a meadow
    One man and his dog...
Jan Oh, sod you and your stupid rotten lawnmower!
Patrick (*bewildered*) She swore at me.
Stuart Yeah—well—they do.
Vicki (*crying out*) Stu! Stuart!

Liz, as a doctor, enters

Liz (*as Doctor*) Mr Cope? I wonder if I might have a word...

Stuart exits, concerned

Caro Rub my back ... oh, that's better ... that's better...
Don I love you...
Chris I love you...
Patrick There ... there...
Paul It's all gone...
Stuart All the pain's going...
Vicki (*weakly*) Stu... Stu...
Stuart All gone ... all gone...

A moment's silence

Liz Oh shit!
Lorraine ...3, 4, 5, 6...

Patrick staggers out, holding his head in one hand and the video recorder in the other, and staggers back in again

Vicki (*as Nurse*) Doctor... Mr Hale has passed out and hit his head on the radiator ... he may need stitches.

Don enters and yells at an unseen someone

Don Come and help my wife.
Stuart He can't help you.
Don For God's sake, he's a doctor, isn't he?
Stuart No mate, he's the resident electrician.

Stuart exits

Don exits

Paul enters

Paul Why isn't anyone doing anything for her!

Paul exits

Stuart enters and stands quietly throughout

Liz I am not a bag you're emptying!

Don enters, looking drained

Vicki (*as Nurse*) It'll be hours yet, Mr Masters.
Don Oh my God.

Don breathes heavily into a portable oxygen mask ... and immediately exits

Patrick We've already said ... she doesn't want any drugs...
Jan Oh, shut up you! Drugs, give me some drugs!
Lorraine Paul!
Paul I'm here, Lolly, I'm here.
Caro Stop giving me running commentaries all the time!
Vicki (*as Nurse*) Would you like an anaesthetic?
Liz No, thanks, I've just put one out ... aahhh!
Jan   One man went to mow
              Went to mow... ohh
Liz (*as Doctor; calling, urgently*) Mr Cope! I need to speak to you urgently ... there are complications, we're losing the heartbeat.
Stuart Coming!

Act II

Stuart exits quickly

Liz (*as Doctor*) Everything's coming along fine, Mrs Sullivan...
Vicki (*as Nurse*) ...it looks like we'll have to induce...
Liz (*as Doctor*) ...well done, you're doing splendidly...
Don ...not long now, darling, not long...
Liz (*as Doctor*) ...we'll have to consider a caesarean...
Jan (*singing drunkenly... under the influence of the drugs*) Ten green bottles
                hanging on the wall
                And if one... ooh
Vicki (*as Nurse*) Blood pressure's high...
Liz (*as Doctor*) Perfect ... there we are ... excellent...
Vicki (*as Nurse*) ...in distress.
Liz (*as Doctor*) ...not long now, Mrs Masters...
Vicki (*as Nurse*) ...rupture the membranes...
Liz (*as Doctor*) ...that's excellent, Mrs Ford...
Vicki (*as Nurse*) ...not dilating...
Liz (*as Doctor*) ...this won't hurt ... won't hurt...
All Voices Push ... push...
Liz I *am* pushing... I *am* pushing!
All Voices Push ... push...
Don She *is* pushing ... she *is* pushing...

The sounds of the women pushing and being encouraged rises

Chris I can see him, I can see!
Paul I love you, Lolly...
Patrick It's fantastic, it's wonderful!
Don I love you, darling, I love you!

As the Lights change so that we can just about make out a circle of figures, the "push push" continues relentlessly, mingled with distorted cries from the women ... and the sounds crescendo ... and there is blinding Light from above ... and we can just make out that the figures are reaching upwards ... and then as the music resolves and the voices and the heartbeat subside, we hear the unmistakable sound of a baby's first cry ... and then the "hospital wall" rises ... and we see all other than Stuart and Vicki are grouped together, the women all in white surgical gowns, each reaching up to where a baby is being held. Stuart and Vicki are away from this group. She kneels on a bed, her head buried in his chest as he comforts her

Don I've known him from the very second he came into the world... I mean the very second...

Jan ...I looked at him and I saw his face and...
Caro ...I realized that he was having her too...
Paul I didn't want to be there ... but it was wonderful...
Helen ...I felt despair and joy and a thousand other things...
Chris ...and then, when I saw her being born...
Patrick ...I cried... I just cried...
Paul The most important thing I've learned...
Lorraine ...is that nothing ever turns out the way you think it will.
Liz He weighs six pounds five ounces. And he's beautiful.

All	Here we are		
	All we've been through		
	End of a journey		
	Starting anew		
	A sense of beginning		
	And what's to be		
	A part of the future		
Men	A part of me		
Women	I'm happy with him	**Men**	Here we are
	I'm happy with me		All we've been through
	What we are		End of a journey
	Is what you see		Starting a new
	We'll see it through		A sense of beginning
	And we'll survive		And what's to be
All	A part of the future		
	Live your own life		

CURTAIN

All On Our Way (curtain call)

FURNITURE AND PROPERTY LIST

Further dressing may be added at the director's discretion

ACT I

On stage: Bed. *On it*: pillows
Table
Chairs
Various notices—including one which reads "Drink Plenty Of Water For The Scan"
Mirror
Golf iron
Light switch
How To Stop Smoking book
Phone

Off stage: Small bunch of freesias (**Chris**)
Pregnancy test tube (**Jan & Patrick**)
Book (**Jan**)
Phone (**Liz**)
Evening paper (**Stuart**)
Fan (**Helen**)
Specialist car magazine (**Stuart**)
"Baby" book, bowl & spoon (**Patrick**)
Breakfast cup (**Don**)
Breakfast cup, letter (**Helen**)
Books (**All Women Except Lorraine**)
Briefcase, manilla file containing letters (**Liz**)
Forms (**Women**)
Polystyrene cup of herbal tea (**Patrick**)
Doctor's clipboard with sheet of paper (**Don**)
New maternity dress (**Caro**)
Electric iron (**Vicki**)
Small towel (**Stuart**)
Small bag of shopping (**Lorraine**)
Huge, rather cheap, teddy bear (**Paul**)
Cordless telephone, glass, bottle of red wine (**Liz**)

                Birthday card (**Helen**)
                Set of keys (**Paul**)
                Expensive suitcase (**Stuart**)
                Glass of champagne, champagne bottle (**Chris**)
                Glass of champagne (**Caro**)
                Knitting (**Stuart**)
                Small stool that used to be pink, blue paint, paintbrush (**Vicki**)

Personal: **Patrick:** handkerchief, sachet
                Women: four-month bulge
                Stuart: packet of cigarettes, lighter
                Vicki: wedding ring suspended on a length of cotton

ACT II

Set: Packages
           Baby doll
           Box
           Newspaper
           Trousers
           Towel
           2 phones
           Pen
           Pad
           Bucket

Off stage: Top hats, canes (**Women & Patrick**)
                Small bulge (**Lorraine**)
                Small bulge (**Vicki**)
                Small bulge (**Liz**)
                Big bulge (**Jan**)
                Big bulge (**Helen**)
                "Sympathy" pregnancy pack (**Patrick**)
                Shoes, exercise clothes (**Liz**)
                Shoes, exercise clothes (**Lorraine**)
                Book (**Helen**)
                Book (**Don**)
                Diary, pen (**Caro**)
                Letter (**Paul**)
                2 mugs of tea (**Liz**)
                Small pamphlet (**Vicki**)
                White nappy (**Don**)
                Duvet (**Caro**)

Furniture and Property List

        Handkerchief (**Chris**)
        Duvet (**Liz**)
        Duvet (**Jan**)
        Tray with bowl of soup and spoon (**Patrick**)
        Children's toys (**Stuart**)
        Bag containing new baby clothes, tiny growsuit (**Caro**)
        Paper (**Chris**)
        Letter (**Paul**)
        Shopping bag (**Lorraine**)
        Headscarf, large paintbrush, aluminium steps (**Vicki**)
        List (**Jan**)
        Birth paraphernalia (**Jan & Patrick**)
        Small suitcase, folded note (**Caro**)
        Small suitcase (**Jan**)
        Large rubber plant, video recorder, bucket, canvas bag containing birth paraphernalia (**Patrick**)
        Overnight bag (**Helen**)
        "Hospital wall" (**SM**)
        Bunch of flowers (**Stuart**)
        Suitcase (**Paul**)
        Portable oxygen mask (**Don**)

Personal: **Stuart:** wad of used banknotes
          Vicki: watch

LIGHTING PLOT

Property fittings required: red light
Various interior and exterior settings

ACT I

To open: Overall general lighting

Cue 1	**Don** turns off the light *Cut lighting on* **Don** *and* **Helen**	(Page 8)
Cue 2	**Don** sits upright, turns on the light *Bring up lighting on* **Don** *and* **Helen**	(Page 8)
Cue 3	**Don**: "Jolly good." *Flash red light*	(Page 19)
Cue 4	**All Women**: "…we'd go through it—a—gain!" *Flash red light*	(Page 35)
Cue 5	**Vicki**: "…fancy going halves on one?" *Flash red light*	(Page 36)
Cue 6	**Liz**: "…and no escape." *Flash red light*	(Page 36)
Cue 7	**Lorraine**: "I'm eighteen." *Flash red light*	(Page 37)
Cue 8	**All**: "And it's moving!" *Fade lights down, focusing on* **Liz**	(Page 46)
Cue 9	**Liz**: "It's mine" *Slowly bring up lights on the others*	(Page 46)

Lighting Plot

ACT II

To open: Overall general lighting

Cue 10	**Voice**: "The show is on!" *Change lights to "un-naturalistic" state*	(Page 81)
Cue 11	**Don**: "I love you, darling, I love you!" *Dim lights*	(Page 91)
Cue 12	Sounds intensify to a crescendo *Bring up blinding light from above*	(Page 91)

EFFECTS PLOT

ACT I

Cue 1	**Don**: "Jolly good" *Buzzer rings*	(Page 19)
Cue 2	**All Women**: "…we'd go through it—a—gain!" *Tannoy calls "Mrs Hale?"*	(Page 35)
Cue 3	**Vicki**: "…fancy going halves on one?" *Tannoy calls "Mrs Beckett"*	(Page 36)
Cue 4	**Liz**: "…and no escape." *Tannoy calls "Mrs Cope?"*	(Page 36)
Cue 5	**Lorraine**: "I'm eighteen." *Tannoy calls "Mrs Ford?"*	(Page 37)
Cue 6	**Lorraine** exits *Tannoy calls "Mrs Spencer"*	(Page 37)
Cue 7	**Don** kisses **Helen** *Phone rings*	(Page 40)

ACT II

Cue 8	Lights change to "un-naturalistic" state *Activity sounds and heartbeat*	(Page 81)
Cue 9	Music resolves *Fade sounds and heartbeat; bring up a baby's first cry*	(Page 91)